MW01703506

& Alive Well

A Path For Living In A Time Of HIV

Peter A. Hendrickson

A volume in the Frontiers of Consciousness series
Series editor, Stanley Krippner

IRVINGTON PUBLISHERS, INC.
NEW YORK

For information write to: Irvington Publishers, Inc.,
Executive offices: 522 E. 82nd Street, Suite 1, New York, NY 10028
Customer service and warehouse: 195 McGregor St, Manchester, NH 03102

Library of Congress Cataloging-in-Publication Data

Hendrickson, Peter (Peter A.)
Alive & well : a path of living in a time of HIV / by Peter Hendrickson
p. cm.
Includes bibliographical references and index.
ISBN 0-8290-2460-3 (paper back)
ISBN 0-8290-2458-1 (cloth)
1. AIDS (Disease)—Alternative treatment. 2. Healing. 3. Yoga.
I. Title. II. Title: Alive and well.
RC607.A26H46 1990
362. 1'969792—dc20 90-43195
CIP

3 5 7 9 10 8 6 4 2

Cover concept by Wayne Mazzotta

Book design and production by

The Bramble Company
Falls Village, Connecticut

Printed in the United States of America

The paper used in this publication meets the minimum requirements of
American National Standard for Information Sciences—
Permanence of Paper for Printed Library Materials,
ANSI Z39.48-1984.

The Author

Peter Hendrickson is a psychologist in private practice in New York City. He received a B.A. from Princeton University in 1974 and Ph.D. from Boston College in 1982. From 1983 to 1986, he served as Director of Psychological Services at the Kennedy Child Study Center in New York. He is a senior teacher at the New York Integral Yoga Institute, where he has led weekly AIDS seminars since 1985. This book is based upon these seminars, called *PATH: Positive Approaches Toward Healing*.

Acknowledgements

Many people have made important contributions to this book. Irving Naiburg has served as both publisher and editor. It was his idea that this book be written, and he has offered sound advice along the way. Rebecca Daniels has contributed much more than her highly skilled word processing and editorial services. Her encouragement and understanding, as well as her belief in the ideas contained here has made everything go smoothly. Tim Allan's kindness and balanced perspective has been a great help. I am very grateful for all he has given. I also want to thank the following people for the essential part they each played in making this book a reality: Nancy Blanford, Larry Bramble, Dr. James Braun, Sister Barbara Dainiak, Peter D'Agostino, Betty D'Agostino, Dr. Mark Finn, Jana Klenburg, Prahaladan Mandelkorn, Wayne Mazzotta, Prema Pleva, Swami Prakashananda, Bert Shaw, Mark Scherzer, Abbey Semel, Garland and Leann Snyder, James Watkins, Mary Willcox, and my parents, John and Betty Hendrickson.

Although the best way to show gratitude to a teacher is to pass on what you have learned to others, I do want to thank Swami Satchidananda. In addition to teaching and exemplifying yoga, I am deeply grateful for his love and belief in me. Stephen Levine's support, compassion, and humanity have been a great gift. Through them I have learned a path of healing which, while it is not easy, is possible.

The people with AIDS I have known have all been important teachers. I thank them all and offer this book to all those who are facing or will face the challenges presented by living with HIV.

Peter Hendrickson
Lake Hill, NY

Table of Contents

Foreword

There are many unanswered questions about acquired immunodeficiency syndrome (AIDS): its origins, its etiology, its prognosis, and its treatment. But there is no question as to the devastating effects that AIDS-related diseases are having on hundreds of thousands of afflicted men and women around the world. In addition, there are millions of people whose bodies are producing antibodies to the human immunodeficiency virus (HIV) that is believed to cause AIDS, and who are at risk for the infections that follow the immune system's breakdown.

Alive *& Well* is written for people whose lives bear the impact of HIV—personally or through a relative, friend, or associate. The book focuses on self-generated healing, especially those approaches taught by Swami Satchidananda, an ecumenical spiritual teacher and Yoga master, whom I first met two decades ago and whom I continue to hold in high esteem.

Peter Hendrickson, the author of *Alive & Well*, wisely differentiates between self-deception and hope, between delusionary thinking and making wise decisions, and between passivity and careful planning. Dr. Hendrickson admits that his proposals lack statistical evidence at the present time. But the suggestions in Alive & Well are certainly amenable to outcome studies. In the meantime, I recently followed a treatment program initiated for a group of prison inmates who were suffering from AIDS-related infections. Isolated in the "AIDS ward" of their New Jersey prison, they followed a regimen outlined by Dr. Philip Hodes, a nutritional counselor. The program resembled Dr. Hendrickson's guidelines—including meditation, visualization, diet, exercise, and positive thinking. At the end of 18 months, the 20 inmates who faithfully followed Dr. Hodes' program were all alive and well. Further follow-up was not possible because many prisoners had been released from jail, and funds were not available for systematic post-treatment interviews.

In examining a threatening and frightening phenomenon, *Alive & Well* identifies such lessons as the need to take charge of our lives, the importance of identifying life priorities, and being true to oneself—to one's feelings, to one's capacity for self-healing, and to one's spiritual nature. Dr. Hendrickson's vividly presented case studies in Alive & Well pay homage to human consciousness, and to Swami Satchidananda's reminder that "the greatest doctor is inside us."

Stanley Krippner, PhD
Saybrook Institute

Introduction

Finding Hope in a Time of Crisis

❖

This book is for all those whose lives have been touched by HIV—whether it be fear about having been exposed to HIV; uncertainty about whether or not to take the HIV-antibody test; anxiety about possible early signs of immune dysfunction; the demands of facing the daily challenges of living with AIDS; or concern about the health of a loved one. It offers practical guidelines for living in a manner which naturally promotes health. This book will also provide you with ways to acquire the emotional, social and spiritual skills you need to face AIDS with courage and hope.

The skills offered in this book facilitate the process of *self-generated healing*. We live in a culture which encourages looking outside ourselves for answers and for fulfillment. Here you will be asked to look within. Those facing AIDS need to be well-informed about the medical, legal, and social aspects of the disease. It is also valuable to learn from the experiences of those who have already lived with AIDS. But we each need to carve out our own response to AIDS. Dr. Michael Lerner, Director of the Commonweal Cancer Help Program, differentiates between healing and curing.[3] Curing refers to fixing or eradicating a symptom. Healing involves a unified effort of the body, mind, and spirit. Healing comes from within and brings about the well-being of the total person. A spiritual and emotional healing can happen even in the absence of a physical cure. Common sense and personal experience may lead you to believe that your state of mind influences your health. However, you may have only limited knowledge in knowing where to begin in gaining that control. You may know what lifestyle changes would promote your health but may be unable or unwilling to follow through.

When suffering goes beyond statistics and touches your life directly, AIDS can become terrifying. For those at risk, any cough, skin blemish or fever can signal the beginning of a life-threatening illness. The diseases which result from a weakened immune system can be extremely painful and make daily life unmanageable. Health insurance is often unavailable. People with AIDS (PWAs) are forced to make critical decisions about their health with little to help them decide who or what will be most effective. Societal indifference coupled with fear about AIDS transmission has caused many to die alone and neglected. In light of all the suffering we have seen and are likely to see, how can we honestly be hopeful about AIDS?

The statistics do not make it easy to be hopeful. Researchers say we are in the early stages of an epidemic which could last at least another decade. The toll it has already taken has been tragic, and every seven minutes another person dies of AIDS. Americans comprise only one fourth of the 250,000 AIDS cases worldwide, according to World Health Organization (WHO) estimates as of this writing.

The grim projections for the future are well-known. Authorities predict 365,000 cumulative AIDS cases in the U.S. and 1,250,000 worldwide by the end of 1992. Current estimates are that between 1 and 1.5 million Americans and 5 million people worldwide are HIV antibody-positive, meaning they have the antibodies to the virus that is thought to cause AIDS.[1,2] A critical question is what proportion of HIV-positive people will eventually develop full-blown AIDS. The prevalent opinion among scientists is that the vast majority of HIV-positive people will die prematurely of

AIDS. However, some scientists are more optimistic, seeing HIV as becoming a manageable chronic infection, in some ways analogous to diabetes.

Not wanting to create the impression that AIDS is easily overcome, I hesitated to use the word hope in the title of this introduction. False hope can be deceiving and even dangerous when it causes irresponsible behavior in caring for one's health. Self-deception and irresponsibility are the problems; hope is not. As we will see, what is most deadly is the despair of living with no hope. There is hope in living in a way which naturally promotes immune strength. And hope comes when we share our pain with others rather than isolate ourselves. The emphasis throughout this book is on *living with* HIV—neither pretending it's not there nor approaching life with panic and despair. This book will help you find value in all life experiences. Many HIV-positive people speak of learning to appreciate life on a moment to moment basis.

I am writing this book from the perspective of a psychologist, as well as a student and teacher of yoga. My practice as a psychologist includes many people who are facing HIV-related concerns. The ideas in this book are derived from different sources—the experiences just mentioned, the teachings of yoga, research in psychoneuroimmunology, and a variety of spiritual as well as psychotherapeutic traditions. Yoga is far more than the physical exercises most people associate with it. It includes the practice of meditation, a broad understanding of health and disease, and guidelines concerning how to make daily life a peaceful and enjoyable experience. The principles of yoga are incorporated in many widely accepted therapies: relaxation training, biofeedback, systematic desensitization, even cognitive therapy. Yoga is neither Indian nor is it a religion. It is a process of naturally bringing health to the body and steadiness to the mind.

It is difficult to learn yoga without a teacher. I am very grateful to have studied yoga for the past seventeen years with Swami Satchidananda, the founder and director of the Integral Yoga Institute. He was born in India in 1914 and first came to the United States in 1966. Although he has a long white beard, wears orange robes and speaks with an accent, I see him as the least "foreign" person I know.

His teachings and counsel address concerns in all areas of life, whether they be about spiritual practices, professional challenges, health, personal relationships, or emotional difficulties. No question is too big or too small. Just recently I spoke with two friends: one was helped by Swami Satchidananda, or Swamiji, in wiring a ceiling light; the other, who was facing the final stages of AIDS, was deeply moved by Swamiji's visit to his home. Wherever life has taken me over these years, I invariably find him several steps ahead—offering guidance, encouragement and comfort. He does not want his students to become dependent upon him. With his characteristic play on words, he says, "Those who stay at the feet of the master will be defeated. It's the teachings, not the teacher. The outer guru is here to guide you to the inner guru." A major focus of Swami Satchidananda's public service has been to help people recognize and experience the underlying unity between different religions. He has also given a great deal of his time to health-related endeavors, working with physicians in establishing cancer and heart programs based on a holistic orientation. These residential facilities have been very effective and are gaining increasing respect in the medical community.

In 1985, the AIDS crisis was very much on my mind. I asked Swami Satchidananda for his suggestions for people concerned about AIDS. He responded with a very strong statement:

> What the doctors say is impossible could be made possible through yoga. Through yoga you are bringing in health. But it is up to you. Lead a strict yogic life, not as a practice but as a treatment. The greatest doctor is inside us, the doctor of doctors—nature's energy. That energy is ready to repair anything and everything, if only we give a little opportunity for that energy to work on us.[4]

He offered suggestions about meditation, yoga practices, diet, and, most importantly, approaching life and illness in a manner which is based on faith, self-empowerment and hope. He described what in this book is called self-generated healing.

I was very encouraged by his words and decided to set up a day-long workshop at the New York Integral Yoga Institute in which these ideas would be presented. Half of the first 50 participants had AIDS, and I quickly became aware of the devastating effect of this disease. One man called me from his home wanting to attend the workshop but unable to come down the four flights of stairs to get out of his apartment. I also had to face my own doubts and fears. Did I really believe that yoga, meditation, dietary and attitude changes could help these people? How was I doing at facing my own fears of illness, death or social isolation? I had experienced how eating well and the yoga practices had given me a profound sense of well-being. But could yoga really do anything for AIDS? Moreover, leading "a strict yogic life" is not easy. I had struggled for years, often unsuccessfully, to live with the discipline which Swamiji was calling for. I doubted if my own life would be an example that could inspire others. Furthermore, I wondered if I had the emotional strength to provide comfort to people who were experiencing such extreme emotional and physical pain.

The workshop was a good beginning, but it immediately became evident that a one-day program was not sufficient to bring about the lifestyle changes that we were encouraging. Weekly seminars were begun in addition to ongoing yoga classes for people with AIDS. We are now in the sixth year. Although no statistical research has been conducted, I am far more convinced of the healing power of yoga and the tremendous effect the mind and emotions have on the body. Swami Satchidananda has said that a residential center is necessary to best implement the ideas of yoga and self-generated healing. In the absence of that facility, our weekly programs continue.

Joe, a PWA and seminar participant, explained that he

approached the self-healing process from a very practical perspective:

> There's a chance that doing these practices will cure AIDS, that I'll lead a full life and become completely healthy. There's a second chance that these practices will lengthen my life until a medical solution becomes available. The third possibility is that I will live my fixed amount of time, but that that amount of time would be much happier and more fullfilling as a result of living in this way. With any of these three outcomes, I'm much better off pursuing the self-healing process.

Joe's doctor encouraged him to do everything possible to keep himself healthy for the two more years that his doctor anticipates it will take before effective medical treatments are available. Joe is working to maximize his health while he awaits medicine in the future.

This book is written so that you can apply the ideas of self-generated healing in your own life. Part One looks at the many challenges faced by a person at risk for HIV-infection—for example, taking the HIV-antibody test; making decisions about treatment; deciding whom to tell. Part One will also discuss interpersonal issues. Friends or family members may be desperately worried about the health of a loved one but not know what to do or say. They are often unable to listen gently to the concerns of a person who is very sick. Similarly, people with AIDS may not know how to ask for comfort or resolve longstanding difficulties with others.

Part Two studies research concerning how thoughts, emotions, and life experiences influence health. You will learn a means of evaluating how you are doing at incorporating the implications of these findings in your daily life.

Part Three explains the steps of self-generated healing—including guidelines on such topics as meditation, imagery exercises, and nutrition. You will be given a framework for a specific course of action towards the illness.

My experience working with people who are facing HIV infection has been in my practice as a psychologist and as an AIDS seminar leader at the Integral Yoga Institute. It is primarily the experiences of the gay population that I am drawing upon. Although other high-risk groups (for example, IV drug users, hemophiliacs, the sexual partners and children of HIV infected individuals) have their own unique concerns, the similarities far exceed the differences. I hope the reader can identify with the experiences of those described here and not dwell on the differences between the various groups affected by AIDS.

There are books on AIDS from many different perspectives—personal, medical, spiritual, historical, cultural, etc. To learn how to face AIDS thoroughly would require studying a curriculum which would include immunology, thanatology, epidemiology, nutrition, spiritual development, and techniques of counseling. No one book can offer what only years of education could provide. I believe this book can help you come to terms with your fears and squarely face the many challenges presented by AIDS and other life-threatening illnesses.

Part I
Making Choices

One

Taking the Test

❖

People at risk for AIDS have many questions. The first questions concern the disease itself: What is AIDS? What are the symptoms? How is it spread? But after HIV, T cells, AZT, KS, PCP, AL721, CMV have all become household abbreviations, one question remains: Should I take the test? Because HIV is seen as the cause of AIDS, a great deal is at stake in learning your HIV status. It is not easy deciding if you are ready to find out.

I have heard many reasons for not taking the test: "There's no treatment available, so what's the point?" "I know I won't take AZT, so why should I learn my HIV status?" "I don't want to know. I'll find out my HIV status if and when I get AIDS." "Sex is important to me. I have safe sex. I don't know who would have sex with me if I found out I was HIV-positive." "Why should I ruin the next several years of my life with the fear that I might be dead in the near future?" "Finding out I'm HIV-positive would cause me so much stress and fear that the news itself would hurt my immune system." "I don't trust that it would remain confidential. My boss or insurance company might find out." By far the most common reason I hear for not taking the test is, "If I test positive I couldn't handle it emotionally. I'm afraid I'd fall apart."

These are all valid concerns. Nevertheless, most AIDS experts recommend testing for those at risk (*New York Times*,

April 24, 1989).[1] These scientists state that knowing HIV-seropositivity is necessary in order to receive medical treatment which could stave off infections and slow down the progress of HIV activity. There are two additional reasons. First, knowledge of HIV status should reduce the likelihood of spreading the virus to others. People who are positive will hopefully be very careful not to transmit the virus. Those who are negative will be highly motivated to stay that way. And, perhaps most importantly, people who test positive will have more incentive to do the hard work of self-generated healing.

Some say that there is no benefit in being tested because no proven HIV treatments are available. But a number of medications have been helpful. Despite the expense and toxicity, those who took AZT are doing better than those in the control group on a placebo. There are prophylactic drugs against AIDS' most lethal disease, pneumocystis caranii pneumonia (PCP). By taking aerosol pentamidine, you greatly reduce the risk of getting PCP. There are other medicines on the market today which some believe to have anti-viral or immune modulating effects. As of this writing, human test trials have been conducted with Compound Q, a drug derived from an herbal extract of Chinese cucumbers, and ddI, a drug similar to AZT.

Knowing your HIV status is important in understanding any other medical problems that might develop. I have seen people whose refusal to know their HIV status has caused denial about a medical problem which required treatment. The result was that their failure to get help made them so sick that they needed a lengthy hospitalization to recover from an illness which would have done much less damage if treated promptly.

In order to keep this epidemic from spreading further, it is imperative that all those who are HIV-positive not transmit the disease to others. *Knowing* rather than *assuming* HIV status puts you in a better position to make responsible decisions concerning your sexual behavior. In response to AIDS, sexual behavior in the gay community has changed dramatically. Because most gay men are now having safer sex (use of condoms, not exchanging body fluids), the rate of transmission of the HIV-virus has been reduced. Nevertheless, people are still taking occasional risks that are potentially life-threatening.

I ask gay men who do not know their own HIV status and are sexually active with more than one partner if they would have sex with a person who is HIV-positive. Many say no. I remind them that, although estimates vary, there may well be a 50% chance that someone who does not know his HIV status is HIV-positive. Often these same people say they are willing to have sex with people who do not know their HIV status. In other words, they are willing to have sex as long as they have a lack of data about the health status of their partner. Others say there is no medical risk in having sex with an HIV-positive person because they will practice safer sex. But many people who say that they only have safer sex will admit that in the heat of the moment the safer sex guidelines are loosened considerably. You risk your life when you have unsafe sex with someone who does not know his or her HIV status. Some people admit that they do not take the HIV test because they fear that positive results would restrict available sex partners. Unless both partners involved have safer sex, the result of not knowing your HIV status can lead to the further spread of AIDS.

Testing positive will give you incentive to do everything to promote your health before you are sick. The AIDS virus can lie dormant in the body for years before it damages the immune system. Rather than bury your head in the sand and let AIDS hit you by surprise, why not face the situation and bring health and well being into all areas of your life? Interestingly, many people are strengthened by the results of taking the HIV antibody status. If you are HIV-positive, you will take your lifestyle—nutrition, stress reduction, relationships, etc.—more seriously. After testing positive, recreational cocaine users often stop taking cocaine. People who drink too much on weekends consume much less alcohol. Those who occasionally had unsafe sex no longer do so. These are important behavioral changes which are health promoting.

Many people do not take the test because they fear their emotional reaction to learning that they are HIV-positive. However, *not* knowing creates an undercurrent of anxiety which is often more harmful and difficult to live with than the reality of testing positive. Taking the test means no longer living with uncertainty. Early in the epidemic leaders in the gay community recommended that you not take the test, but assume that you are HIV-positive. This would only make sense if, being uncertain about your HIV status, you are able to muster the determination that self-generated healing requires. Rare is the person with that determination about an unconfirmed medical condition. Many people live very depressed lives, assuming that they are seropositive because of the health of previous sexual partners, only to take the test and find out that they are HIV-negative. They had been living with a sense of doom which was based on a false assumption. Conversely, I know someone who had assumed that he was HIV-positive because of a misunderstanding during a conversation with his doctor. Armed with the certainty that he had the HIV virus, he stopped taking recreational drugs, discontinued having sexual contacts which were either unsafe or anonymous, began a yoga and meditation practice, and attended seminars on facing AIDS with hope. Then, two years later, his doctor told him that in fact he was negative and had misunderstood what had been said. Over the next several months, this person resumed anonymous sexual behavior, smoked pot sometimes through entire weekends, started drinking again, and could not be found at the Yoga Institute. Unfortunately, many of us do not have the discipline to follow the path of self-generated healing unless we know what is at stake.

Another reason for not taking the test is a fear about confidentiality. You can take the test either confidentially or anonymously. With confidential testing, the doctor says he will not tell anyone. With anonymous testing you go with a false name and do not give your address, phone number or social security number. But remember that medical care in America is not confidential. Any doctor could have his medical records subpoenaed by an insurance company in order to settle health, disability or life insurance claims. Anonymous testing centers do exist where no names are used. If you see any risks in confidential testing, take the test anonymously.

Before you take the test, I recommend that you have a plan *in writing* about what you will do if you test positive. To whom will you talk? To whom will you not talk? I know one man who was so upset by the news of being told he was HIV-positive that he told his immediate supervisor at work. She in turn told her supervisor, who told the president of the company. Fortunately, he has not lost his job, but has been left feeling uneasy about how the news is perceived by the hierarchy in the company. Avoid putting yourself in a situation where you might act impulsively when you hear news of being positive. Some people tell their parents, others do not. Some want to be alone, others with friends. Be sure there is at least one person with whom you can discuss your feelings freely and regularly. Choose a course of action which will provide you comfort and in which you will be able to face your feelings rather than let these same feelings overwhelm you. The next chapter provides further discussion of handling the news of being HIV-positive.

Most people at risk for HIV infection have heard sound reasons for taking the test. Still, many remain afraid and do not take the difficult step of finding out their HIV status. Taking the test is a very personal decision. No one can make this decision for you. You may need more time before you are ready. The ideas in this book will still be helpful even if you decide against being tested at this time. Nevertheless, there can be very real benefits in finding out. Be careful not to let an important medical decision be based on fear.

If You are HIV-negative

If you find out that you are negative, an obvious reaction might be to breathe a sigh of relief and proceed with your life without any fear. But it is not that simple. You are faced with the likely outcome of witnessing the deaths of countless friends as this epidemic continues to take its toll, making you a survivor of a plague which will have a profound impact on your life and on our society. I do not recommend indiscriminately telling people HIV-negative results. The news can cause barriers between those who are HIV-negative and positive and generate uneasiness in those who are silent about being HIV-positive.

Being HIV-negative raises questions about future sexual involvements. Should you only have sexual contact with people who are HIV-negative? How can you trust that they truly know their results? Even if you do trust them, what is the possibility that they have sero-converted (been exposed to the HIV virus and subsequently developed antibodies since taking the test)? Is it possible that you may test HIV-positive a few months from now? Studies do show a very low seroconversion rate: approximately one percent of those who test HIV-negative later test HIV-positive. However, a recent study reported that some sexually active gay men tested HIV-negative for three years after exposure to the virus before subsequently testing HIV-antibody-positive. In other words, three years passed before they developed antibodies to the virus. Doctors had previously told patients that they would test seropositive within six months after exposure. This study suggests that those in high risk groups who test negative should think seriously about a lifestyle that naturally promotes immunity.

You must decide how you define safer sex and what chances, if any, you are willing to take. Do not be ashamed to refuse to engage in behavior that you might regret later. It is advisable to avoid circumstances which might cause you to have poor judgment—for example, dating people who have unsafe sex, drinking too much alcohol, or going to sexually active bars.

You might find that after testing negative you experience what is called survivor's guilt: "Why should I live while so many others die?" An alternative response to negative HIV results might be to learn even more about AIDS and do AIDS volunteer work. Testing negative does not mean that your concerns are over, certainly not for anyone living in a community where so many others have AIDS.

Two

Facing HIV with Courage and Hope

❖

If you are HIV-positive

What happens if you learn you are HIV-positive? Your reaction in large part depends on what you are expecting. You might expect to test positive if one or more of your sexual partners, from days before anyone knew about safer sex, is HIV-positive or has AIDS. But the circumstances differ from person to person. One man was shocked to learn that he was HIV-positive after engaging in no high-risk behavior since testing negative the year before. He concluded that he was exposed to the virus during a sexual contact a few weeks before the initial test. Another man told me that for him and his friends the first reaction to testing positive is "to cancel magazine subscriptions and to give your clothes away." Another man said, "Testing positive confirmed my sense that being gay is awful." Your reaction to being positive also depends on your overall health. If you look and feel fine, it may be hard to believe that your life is threatened by a microorganism that is causing you no current symptoms. However, if you have been sick for some time, the news of being HIV-positive may explain your recent illnesses. Whatever your expectations, it is likely that you will have a wide range of feelings—sorrow, fear, indifference, anger, peace of mind—all in the course of a day.

Some people react to HIV-positive results with severe emotional reactions, including crippling anxiety or incapacitating depressions. My experience as a psychologist has been that these acute reactions diminish over a few weeks time when people receive effective counseling and are given information about others in the same circumstances.

It helps if you have already made a plan about whom you will discuss the test results with. You have no obligation to tell your employers, friends, or anybody in particular. You do not need to say that you have taken the test at all. A different response is recommended with sexual partners of the past, present or future. To minimize spread of the virus, it is best to confidentially tell previous sexual partners. Similarly, current partners have every right to know, as do people you may sleep with in the future. Some say that as long as you have safer sex, there is no need to tell a sexual partner about being HIV-positive. I have known people who have had sex with someone, have not told the partner, then wanted to call the person to see him again, but did not do so because they were afraid of telling them that they had sex without disclosing HIV-status. If they felt so strongly that there was nothing to hide, why were they afraid to call the person for another date?

You will see the world through different eyes after learning about being HIV-positive. When talking about events in the future, a relative going to college ten years from now, or about the year 2000, you will wonder if you will be alive then. You will no longer assume that you will survive your parents and live into your eighties.

If you are HIV-positive, find a doctor. Don't wait until you are sick. Some people want to change their doctor because they are angry at him or her for being the messenger of bad news. If you are not happy with your doctor, consider finding another one, but not because he told you a medical fact. Some symptoms require immediate medical attention, for example, blurred vision which does not get prompt treatment could lead to blindness caused by cytomegalovirus.

Herpes zoster can be treated quickly with Acyclovir before turning into a serious case of shingles. Prophylaxis for PCP is effective. For all these reasons, it is good to watch your health carefully and to be in regular contact with your doctor.

Unfortunately, many physicians treating AIDS, especially in New York City, have practices which are completely full. These doctors spend each day telling people whether they are likely to live or die. Sometimes this news is not given with much sensitivity. Do not expect that all the comfort you need regarding being HIV-positive will come from your doctor. Most physicians treating AIDS are under enormous stress. With a disproportionate number of patients hospitalized and facing death, these doctors are overworked, overwhelmed, and at times, short-tempered. One mother told me of being with her son at the hospital when the doctor told him that he was extremely sick with AIDS. "I remember him looking up from his hospital bed at his doctor, almost with a pleading disbelief. 'Can this really be so?'" When doctors see these faces of pleading disbelief all day, their own defenses may make them seem distant and unavailable. Because of this, it is imperative that you have a support system which includes, but extends beyond, your doctor visits.

If you are totally asymptomatic, your HIV-status may seem unreal. As a result, you may not see the harm in overexposing yourself to the sun, not getting enough rest, or failing to eat well. Remind yourself again and again that your health is the topmost priority. No relationship, job, vacation is more important than living in a way which will keep you healthy. Greg went to his doctor last November because of flu-like symptoms. On the return visit the next week the doctor informed him that not only was he HIV-positive but his low T-4 cells caused him to be given a diagnosis of AIDS Related Complex (ARC). The doctor recommended AZT. Greg's flu symptoms cleared without any medication, leaving him feeling fine but knowing that lab tests had revealed a possibly fatal health problem. Within a few days, Greg reimmersed himself in his hectic urban life—with two jobs and many other commitments that left him with little time to sit still. I suggested that he make time for himself to reflect on what was happening in his life. His reply expresses the often contradictory feelings of someone who is HIV-positive yet still feels healthy.

> Sometimes I'm afraid to think... because it's too frightening.... Right now it's still not real because I'm healthy.... I go to the doctor, I talk to him. I know my blood level. But it's still not a reality. I have hope that something will happen within medicine.... And then I think about my son [age 12]. How am I ever going to tell him about this? ... I know a half dozen people who have died in the past week. That doesn't help.... Part of me says this is still not real. It's not that I'm in denial, but part of me is in denial.

Many people report HIV-related fatigue. It is not easy to determine whether the inertia is caused by a physical problem related to HIV or is emotionally based. Often both mind and body are weakened by being HIV-positive. I knew one man with ARC who was able to work six hours at a time. Afterwards, he was so exhausted he would sleep until the next morning and then through the entire weekend. However, his energy went up markedly when he started caring for himself: eating well, not drinking alcohol or taking recreational drugs, attending a support group, and educating himself about the possibilities of survival. He ended one unhealthy relationship, found a new boyfriend, and pursued old interests which he had neglected for years. Another man who had AIDS had been bedridden for days. Yet when he got a two week freelance job, he was up early in the morning, eager for work, happy to feel useful again.

Work is a basic form of self-expression. A great many long-term AIDS survivors are actively working in AIDS organizations. Work enables participation in your community and in the lives of others. Don't take being HIV-positive as a reason to give up the opportunity for satisfaction that work can provide. Dr. Jeffrey Greene, a physician at New York University Medical Center, has formed an organization, Multitasking Systems, which provides office employment for PWAs in New York City.

Barry had had a successful career in the theatre. He remained relatively healthy for years with AIDS when he was directing and producing a show which had productions overseas. The show closed in June. Another show which he had planned to be part of was cancelled in July. He became sick in August and died in September.

The Diagnosis

Even though you may have suspected it for months, it is very sad and sobering to hear your doctor tell you that you have AIDS. Many see this as the point of no return. Somehow they were able to remain hopeful being HIV-positive. But the AIDS diagnosis removed the last glimmer of hope. As Luis Pallacios-Jimenez, a PWA, said, "You may feel life isn't worth living after diagnosis. I learned this was only a feeling and this feeling, like all feelings, shall pass."[1] Christopher Sherman, also a PWA, writes, "Get angry, get mad, get enraged. But whatever you do, get control of your situation as soon as possible."[2] Being diagnosed is about choices—choices about treatment, and most importantly, choices about how you relate to the news.

As Christopher Spence, author of *AIDS: The Time to Reclaim Our Power*, writes:

> Every moment we can choose our point of view. We can choose to see AIDS as a grim crisis for humanity or as an extraordinary opportunity, individually and collectively, to move forward. We can allow it to confirm our powerlessness, despair, hopelessness ..., or we can use it as the springboard from which to make the oldest most graceful leap towards living the life of our dreams and getting our world exactly right.[3]

Often people see having AIDS as a sign of failure. They are embarrassed about the way it was transmitted and what others may think about that. They are terrified about being seen with lesions or other evidence of illness. Some who have followed a holistic plan of self-healing feel that their efforts were in vain, that they may have subconsciously caused the illness. They may feel betrayed by their holistic efforts—in a sense, let down by visualization exercises or a macrobiotic diet. They might give up, angry, hopeless, and without any alternative course of action.

There is a connection between the mind and body. But that connection does not mean that if you have hope, are true to yourself, minimize stress, etc., that you will never get sick and die. Michael Callen says that *all* the long term AIDS survivors he has known have had hope, but many hopeful PWAs have died. You are responsible *to* your AIDS, not *for* your AIDS. As Stephen Levine, author and workshop leader who has worked with the dying for many years, says:

> I've seen too many 95-year-old widows strapped in wheelchairs in convalescent homes praying every day to die and not dying, in fact, losing their faith in God because God won't take them. Every cell is soaked with a desire to die, but it's not enough. On the other hand, I've seen people who work so hard using every healing practice, techniques that are very difficult for them to undergo, who do everything they can to stay in the body, and still die. They're not failures. And ideas like "You choose to live or you choose to die" are half-truths which, taken deeper, can be very valuable, but left on the surface can be very destructive.
>
> The idea that you're responsible for your cancer has caused as much suffering as any idea I've ever seen. We're not responsible for our cancer; we're responsible *to* our cancer. If you find pain in the body and say "I'm responsible for this pain," then judgment is

> liable to encircle and encrust that pain, and that very resistance amplifies suffering. But if you're responsible *to* your pain, then you can bring it into your heart....
>
> I know holistic doctors who, having gotten cancer, have said, "My gracious, I've told people things, said things off the top of my head, that now I see aren't so. I have to open my heart to my cancer. I have to be responsible to it. There's no blame. Who knows?" I think "don't know" is far better to work with than causation. I've seen too many saints die of illness.[4]

You also have choices about whom you tell and when. You can tell people face to face, on the phone, or in a letter. You can take several months informing people. Do this in a way in which you feel that you are maintaining some control over the situation and all the feelings that will surface.

You need to know what you are feeling before you can release it. It's natural to feel cheated at the prospect of dying during your twenties or thirties. However, the anger about being cheated can create a barrier or armor around the pain about AIDS, when what is most needed is a gentle awareness. One man told me of his anger and fear about having AIDS:

> I resent the interruption in my life. I resent the change in my life. Now I have to live with the very real possibility that I am 30-years-old, and I could die a very painful death within the next year. I put up this brave front to show that I can deal with it, but I can't. Peter, it's just not fair. I feel so cheated. I went through life with all this potential about where I was headed. I feel I'm never going to have any peace of mind, and I'll die an awful death. I want somebody to love me, but there's not someone who can love me enough to make me feel that I count and that I'm not this horrible diseased per-

son. I don't want to die. I'm afraid to die. I just don't want to die.... But AIDS is a part of me. I can't put it outside. It's inside of me.

Not surprisingly, the dreams of PWAs are often about AIDS. You might dream about symptoms spreading, hospitalizations, personal rejection, death. Don't be frightened by these dreams or see them as predictions about future suffering. Try not to view them as signs of failure or as indications that your entire mind is not hopeful. The psyche is doing its work. There is bound to be a lot of fear, not only in the conscious mind, but also in the subconscious. Try to understand and accept the fear that the dream is representing, but not to the point of dwelling on frightening images. You may also have beautiful dreams which provide you with guidance and inspiration. Treasure these dreams. As you develop your relationship with your inner guide, it is not uncommon to have specific dreams with suggestions for healing.

Symptoms

Michael Lerner observes that long-term cancer survivors resemble veterans of combat in Vietnam or Korea. Many soldiers die of fright and surrender during their first year of battle. Survivors develop skills to persevere and have extraordinary intuition. Lerner's Commonweal Cancer Care Program seeks to codify these skills and pass them on to newly diagnosed cancer patients. In the case of AIDS, PWAs and HIV-positive individuals have a community where these survival skills of perseverance are being passed on to more newly diagnosed individuals. For example, a recently published book, *Surviving and Thriving with AIDS: Collected Wisdom, Volume II*, written by and for PWAs, is a classic in this effort to pass on wisdom from one PWA to another. The book is invaluable, both for the self-empowerment it offers and the specific ideas about AIDS-related conditions. (Information about how to obtain this and other books is contained in the bibliography.) I have never seen two cases of AIDS that are identical. The symptoms, emotions, social network, length of time, etc. are all evidence of each person's uniqueness. Nevertheless, whatever you are feeling, or whatever your symptoms are, someone has probably been through it before and has written about it in a PWA journal or is participating in a support group which you might find helpful.

HIV symptoms can seem relatively harmless at first—a rash, lymph swellings, slight diarrhea. Daily life is not affected. Relationships, work, continue as usual. The major significance of these early symptoms can be that they are harbingers of more severe difficulties that lie ahead.

When AIDS progresses, the diseases which result from a weakened immune system can be incapacitating and extremely painful. The bodies of some PWAs are covered with lesions. Others have had severe diarrhea for months. Many are weak and unable to walk. Some PWAs lose their vision. Many experience impairments in mental functioning. AIDS has caused brain damage, liver disease, kidney disease. It is often extremely painful.

Todd, diagnosed with AIDS one year ago, sounded terrified when he called last week. He had been coughing and feared a recurrence of PCP. He went on to say that he had recently lost control of his bowels. "I hate it. I won't live this way. I'm thirty years old. My grandmother didn't have this problem until she was ninety-five. It's disgusting." I asked him if he would be willing to tell his lover how he was feeling. "No, I can't do that. I'm too ashamed." Todd needed to vent his feelings of anger and fear. The next day he was willing to talk with his lover and began to approach his symptoms with more acceptance.

If at all possible, get through the nightmare times as quickly and painlessly as possible. Get treatment, get to the hospital, do what has to be done. But be aware of the difference between pain and suffering. Dr. Kathleen Foley of New York's Memorial Sloane-Kettering Cancer Center explains that, "Pain is a physical hurt; suffering is an emotional hurt."[5] Pain comes from the tumor itself, while suffering comes from the knowledge that you have AIDS. When soldiers' injuries were so severe that the injury was a ticket home from the war, these soldiers experienced less suffering than others whose injury was less severe and would result in a return to combat.

Do your best to learn to *live with* symptoms. Set specific goals for daily life: e.g., going out for walks, attending a support group, seeing a movie. Try not to let the disability be disproportionate to your disease. And, if at all possible, do not let your lifestyle revolve exclusively around the illness role. Avoid a perpetual search for new medical care. Have social outings where you do not discuss your illness.

AIDS-related problems can cause excruciating pain. When medication is appropriately administered, you do not usually have to live with intense, ongoing pain. Some doctors use a three-stage step-ladder with pain medicine. First is mild pain killers such as Tylenol or aspirin. If the pain persists, a mild opiate narcotic such as codeine is prescribed. If the pain increases, a strong narcotic drug such as morphine or dilaudid could be used. Many people suffer extreme pain for months as a result of a variety of AIDS complications. The situation may seem hopeless until the pain is alleviated dramatically when the medication is changed.

Physical pain lessens when feelings are expressed and when you learn meditative skills for dealing with it. Meditation and relaxation techniques are taught at behavioral medicine clinics in hospitals across the country. In his book, *Who Dies?*, Levine offers five guided meditations on pain: "Opening Around Pain; Deep Relaxation: Filling the Body with Silence; Exploring Pain; Exploring Awareness Beyond the Body; Letting it All Float Free."[6] These meditations enable you to face pain. In the process of this exploration, pain often dissolves. Be careful not to get caught in thoughts that intensify pain. For example, "Is this pain caused by a tumor?" Or, "How long will this last?" Try to focus your awareness on the pain, observing it in a relaxed moment to moment manner. To an individual who has been numbing pain with pills throughout his life, the idea of a meditation on one of the most acute pains he has ever experienced might seem preposterous, even infuriating. The truth is the pain is subjectively experienced and can be lessened without taking addicting and mentally-disorienting medications.

Clinical findings suggest that it is preferable for patients to take charge of administering their own pain medication.[7] When they are given their daily limit of pills each morning and are instructed to use them as needed, these patients take less pain medication than when it is administered on a prescribed schedule during the day. Also, research has shown that exercise is helpful with pain patients. You are encouraged to do whatever physical activity is possible. Finally, as Swami Satchidananda says, "When you don't want pain, it pains more. When you accept it, it pains less. Pain will not be a pain if you understand it and accept it."

Making Decisions About Treatment

Anyone who says he has *the* treatment for AIDS has not been around long enough to see people die regardless of their treatment. The most difficult part of having AIDS is making critical decisions with so few facts about what if anything will help. Next to taking the HIV test, the big decision concerning AIDS today is whether or not to take AZT—the most frequently prescribed drug for treating HIV infection. Major studies have shown that those taking AZT have remained healthier than those on a placebo. However, AZT is also very toxic and very expensive. Dr. Barry Gingell, formerly a physician at GMHC in New York City, wrote: "While it may prolong life in the short term, AZT creates its own set of serious hematologic problems, which may in fact contribute to the disease rather than moderate it."[8]

Others take the position that if it's not broken, don't fix it. Currently, people who are basically asymptomatic have been taking AZT. The problem with AIDS is that it is hard to know when a minor problem could be about to erupt into a more major one and therefore needs immediate treatment. I know one woman who has had ARC for eight years. Her doctor wanted her to take AZT and said that it was her denial that made her hesitate. Finally, she relented and began taking AZT, going against her own instinct. She had a severe toxic reaction which required hospitalization. She very much regretted agreeing to take the drug. However, others have taken AZT and say that it has improved their health with relatively minor side effects.

It is easy to say, "Trust your doctor," but it is not that simple. When PWAs get together they learn that their respective doctors sometimes recommend different treatments for the same problem. They understandably wonder whose doctor is right and know that their life may be at stake. Try to find a doctor you trust—preferably, one with experience in treating AIDS. Educate yourself as much as possible. Get in touch with your own sense of what course of action you want to pursue. Discuss your reservations if your doctor recommends treatment that does not feel right. When your friends, your intuition and your doctor do not agree, seek to resolve the conflict before you follow a course of action which does not feel right.

Facing Others

If you have AIDS, it is useful to look at how you are relating to others in regard to your illness. On the physical level, the lesions and weight loss often caused by AIDS can make you apprehensive to be seen by family and friends.

Take time to think about the people in your life. Whom are you avoiding? Why? Is anyone avoiding you? Can anything be done about that? What are you afraid to say? What feelings are you not letting yourself feel? With whom are you open or closed? In a given relationship, are you willing to open just a little bit more? How would that increased openness be expressed? What do you gain by being closed or being open? Many people find that the courage and hope they need to face AIDS effectively comes only after letting others know their sorrow and helplessness.

As the disease progresses, people with AIDS may find a change in response from their friends. This phenomenon is called anticipatory grief, meaning the emotional withdrawal of others when faced with the reality of the death of a loved one. One person with AIDS said:

> A lot of my friends enjoyed taking me out to dinner when I wasn't so sick. But now I'm in too much pain and I'm just not able to leave the house. These same friends are not interested in just coming over here and sitting with me.... My sister knows how to be with me. Her presence means so much. She doesn't have to say anything. Once we just looked at each other and burst into tears. I will miss her so.

I have seen many PWAs place great emphasis on finding a lover. It becomes their primary focus. This is understandable; AIDS is not easy to face alone. However, the topmost priority needs to be healing. A romantic pursuit could distract you from being responsible to yourself at this time. It is great to go out and make social contacts, but don't forget to find intimacy with yourself and with those already in your life.

Facing Death

> ***Dharma:*** *And what is the greatest marvel?*
> ***Yudhishthira:*** *Each day, death strikes and we live as though we're immortal. This is what is the greatest marvel.*
>
> From Mahabaharta, by Jean Claude Carriere
> (translated by Peter Brook).[9]

We live in a society which denies death. We put rouge on the cheeks of dead bodies, and we seek to keep death outside of our awareness in a way which reflects the falseness in our society. Dr. Mark Finn, a Buddhist psychologist, talks about false magic and true magic. False magic comes from the thrills in life which are based on fleeting phenomena and the denial that our bodies grow old, get sick and die. True magic is the magic which comes when we accept the impermanence of life and from that acceptance find beauty.

The books I have read on death and dying invariably begin with the statement that the book is not about death, but about life. They say that the way to prepare for death is to be open to life. In other words, the best preparation for life is a whole-hearted openness to the present moment. "If you are here now, you will be there then," says Stephen Levine.[10]

When asked what they would do if they were told they had a terminal illness, many people say they would head off on a luxury vacation as they charged their credit cards up to the limit. In fact, people very rarely take this proverbial trip to the beach. A more pressing feeling upon diagnosis is a desire to deepen oneself emotionally and prepare for death. People often regret living a life where priorities were misplaced and grudges held for too long.

You begin the grieving process by learning to let go. Most of us desperately try to cling to positive experiences and scheme to avoid adverse ones. By holding on so tight, we miss out on everything but occasional fleeting moments of joy. A life which has been open to sorrow as well as to joy will be a life which is prepared for death. Each day you can prepare for death and, in so doing, truly begin to enjoy life by accepting change and all life experiences. This includes accepting the disappointments you have tried to block out of your consciousness. In other words, by accepting the fact that you were not first in your class, that you did not have the nicest house in the neighborhood, that someone else got the job, that other people are better looking, that you were not in the in-crowd in high school or at the bars, that you have been rejected in love, that people you loved have died, that you could die with so much undone, that 192,000 people will die today (many seemingly before their time)—accepting all these things, being willing to live with these events, are all preparations for death.

There comes a time in an illness where, as one man with AIDS wrote, "I've reached the point where optimism about my health would have become self-denial." Some people fear that by letting go they will die; if they are completely at peace, they fear they will be released into death. As a result, they cling to life. In fact, the more we open our clenched fist, the more the life force can come through us. There is a big difference between a genuine openness to whatever life gives and wanting death. A man came to my office thrilled about a dream he had had a few days before. In the dream, he took a train which brought him to heaven. He stayed up for several hours that night experiencing that he was in heaven. He said that he felt a timelessness and an identification with his spirit. He even woke up his lover that night saying, "I took the number 7 train to heaven!" He was still feeling the ecstasy of the dream when he spoke to me a few days later. This dream led him to decide to discontinue his efforts to heal his body because, "It doesn't matter. I'm not my body." Seeing his experience as valid, I accepted his explanation. When I told Swami Satchidananda about this man's experience, he suggested that I may have been mistaken in not encouraging him to continue with his efforts to promote his health. "As long as there is life in the body, you do everything to make it healthy." When I questioned him about the yoga teaching saying that clinging to life in the body is an obstacle to self-realization, Swamiji said that he was not talking about *clinging* to life, but *caring* for the body and promoting its health. Swamiji was saying that this person should have continued his healing plan regardless of the dream. In this case we are not talking about radical life support measures, but caring for oneself and simultaneously accepting what happens.

What do you want to do with the time remaining? What unfinished business do you have? With whom do you need to make peace? What debts are unpaid?

The question of suicide needs consideration. If you are faced with months and months of excruciating pain and see no possibility of survival, it is logical to ask why you would want to keep on living. But it is not a decision to be made impulsively. If you see no option, no alternative to a life of extreme pain or living in a vegetative condition, you might want to choose suicide. The Hemlock Society provides information to help people who are considering this alternative. Swami Satchidananda, however, is emphatic in advising against suicide:

> Never, never, never think that it is a good way out. You are not going to escape your pain by committing suicide. Your pain is your friend. If you commit suicide, you are murdering your own friend. When you understand the truth about pain, half its strength is diminished. Have faith in a higher power. Face the difficulties. Be brave.

Suicide often leaves enormous pain for the loved ones of the person who has taken his or her life. "Everyone lives with a skeleton in their closet. When they kill themselves, they become the skeleton in everyone else's closet," says Levine. My experience has been that when people are given the opportunity to talk about their pain and feelings of isolation, they often no longer want to kill themselves. Sharing the pain and horror of facing AIDS makes it so much more manageable. In the sharing PWAs find the dignity and meaning to be found in all life experiences. As one man, diagnosed with AIDS one year ago, told me, "For me, AIDS is about making it through the hard times. When I found out I had PCP for the second time, I wanted to kill myself. Then I realized that there were treatments for the medical problems, but the *despair* was what could kill me."

The two things that people with terminal illnesses fear the most are extreme pain and emotional and physical isolation. Many people have said to me that they do not fear death as much as they fear more physical pain. They fear dying alone. Stephen Levine reports that of the thousands of people who have discussed their near-death experiences with him, *none* have described it as lonely. Death is an experience of expansion and release, not one of constriction or isolation.

Very often people feel emotionally isolated even when there are loved ones nearby. Many speak of the "conspiracy of silence" that surrounds death. I have known many people to die without ever discussing the topic—certainly not writing a will or making plans for a funeral. It may be difficult to deal with the reality of one's own death, but failing to write a will creates unnecessary problems for those left behind.

John, a PWA, shared at a seminar that keeping his life in order is an important part of his healing. This includes letting go of some material possessions. "I have a friend who loves my leather jacket. I gave it to him. It didn't mean I was giving up and dying. The giving made me feel alive and free."

Although people say they would prefer to die at home, four out of five die in the hospital. Dr. James Braun, a New York physician with extensive AIDS experience, believes that those who have accepted the likelihood of their death are often able to make arrangements so they can die at home. Talk with your caregivers about how you would like to die. Who should be there? Would you want to hear any particular music, or poems, or scripture? Many religious traditions place tremendous importance on the nature of our thoughts at the moment of death. Buddhist teachings state that the particular thought at the moment of death influences subsequent births. Gandhi repeated, "Ram, Ram, Ram," a Hindu name for God, as he was assassinated. Many with AIDS die in peace. Unfortunately, others die struggling. In some cases, futile life support measures are employed. Dr. Bernie Siegel, a surgeon and well-known author, believes that it is not coincidental that most hospitalized patients die between midnight and four a.m. Because they are alone, with no visitors and a limited hospital staff, they can die peacefully. Stephen Levine says that during the moments preceding, and even following, death, we can perform a great service to the dying person by gently encouraging him or her to let go and trust—in light, in love, in their experience of release.

Often those left behind experience a profound sense that their departed loved one is at peace. One woman, who had been in a coma for weeks, came out of the coma, looked at her husband and said, "Thank you. I love you. It's time for me to leave." She then leaned back and died.

There are two basic understandings of death. One is that

death is the end. The other is that life survives death. The yogic thinking is that the soul existed before and continues after death. It occupies a body, but it is not that body. My personal experiences have led me to the conviction that a part of us survives death. This part could be called our spiritual awareness. However, this understanding must be experienced, not merely a belief. It is helpful to read books on the subject, e.g. by Elizabeth Kubler-Ross or Stephen Levine, among others. Any learning about near-death experiences would be helpful in gaining a knowledge that will strengthen you and reduce your fear.

Three

Caring for Someone with AIDS

❖

If current projections prove to be accurate, millions of lives will be touched by AIDS. The person with AIDS might be a friend or lover, someone in your immediate or extended family, neighborhood, or work place. AIDS poses special challenges to the caregivers. Although we can learn from people who have provided care to those with other terminal diseases, there are aspects of AIDS which make it unique: a long incubation period with no symptoms for years, the incidence of AIDS in so many young people, and the stigma of homosexuality or intravenous drug use associated with AIDS. Through caring for someone with AIDS, your life may never be the same. You will have an opportunity to learn a great deal and experience intimacy and authenticity in ways which you might previously have thought impossible.

Very ill with a cancer which had metastasized, the father of a friend returned home to spend his last days with his wife and son. As the man's health continued to deteriorate, the end of the son's graduate school semester drew near. The mother told her son that it would be fine for him to return to school to study for exams. "Mom," he replied, "it's an honor to care for Dad at this time." His mother said later that, "He cared for his father not because he thought it would raise him to another level, but because it was the thing to do." Another man recently learned that a friend since early childhood had just been diagnosed with AIDS. After the initial shock, he helped his friend find the necessary medical care, face family members and tell them of the illness. During a lengthy hospitalization, he emptied bedpans and wiped his friend when he lost control of his bowels. "I feel that I have been given a test and I'm passing," he told me. These two examples illustrate that "doing what needs to be done" is the best means for being at peace with yourself and fulfilling your responsibility to others. When we fail to respond to a friend who has AIDS, we are left with remorse and an uneasy sense of unfinished business.

Begin by considering your place among the people caring for a particular person with AIDS. PWAs often have one or two primary caregivers. What role does the person with AIDS want you to play? Open communication between all those involved is likely to improve the quality of experience for everyone and prevent unnecessary feelings of guilt or resentment.

Facing Your Own Fears

An immediate reaction for friends and caregivers is the fear of contagion—the possibility that they could get AIDS by caring for someone with AIDS. You may have had meals and spent a lot of time with this person who has probably been HIV-positive for years. But the knowledge that he has AIDS often brings with it an immediate anxiety. Assurances from the medical profession that AIDS is not transmitted by casual contact have helped lessen these fears. But even if you are not worried, you may have friends who think it dangerous to put yourself in close proximity with someone who has AIDS. There are no incidents of AIDS occurring for the non-sexually involved roommates of a person with AIDS. Despite this, people remain uneasy.

Underneath the fear of contagion are other concerns which do not have such easy answers. Sister Patrice Murphy,

Supportive Care Coordinator at St. Vincent's Hospital in New York City, asks that AIDS caregivers look at suffering and their own history of physical illness.[1] It is also necessary to consider any unsettling thoughts and feelings you have about sexuality, including homosexuality; drug abuse; social isolation and rejection; and death and dying. It is safe to say that most people in our society are not comfortable hearing about one man's love and sexual attraction for another man. We have little sympathy for the social and psychological forces which cause drug addiction. Few people have the courage to cope with the uneasiness and hostility they might face in their community if they were to have a person with AIDS live in their home. There is tremendous pain in seeing the physical deterioration and death of a loved one. Hardly anyone I have known is comfortable with all these topics. Some gay people may be relaxed talking about sexuality but not death. Others may be experienced with death and dying, but are very uneasy about sexuality. Remember that caring for someone with AIDS will be on-the-job training.

What is most important is your willingness to be of service to the other person. My cousin, after years of hesitation, finally told his aunt that he was gay. At the same time he told her he had AIDS-Related Complex. She promptly went out to get books about AIDS and homosexuality. By his side throughout what she referred to as the "precious days" of his illness, she once asked in disbelief, "How could he ever *think* I would stop loving him?"

You will also be faced with many questions about your own mortality, about uncertainty and the randomness of life. Why him and not me? Another response is a sense of helplessness—not knowing what to do or say and feeling inadequate to face the challenge. There are support groups for caregivers which should help you with barriers you might have to face as you attempt to be a compassionate caregiver. Psychologist Brenda Lukeman beautifully states the way to be a caregiver: "Become steady and simple and learn how to extend a truly helping hand."[2]

Living with Uncertainty

If you are a primary caregiver of a person with AIDS, realize that for a period of time your life will be taken over. Months of calm may precede a medical emergency. Your personal life as you have known it will be restricted. Do not forget your own needs for support. Keep going to exercise class, spend time with your own friends, get out and do what you enjoy. If possible financially, you might want to employ home health care personnel to ease the burden. Even more important than hired home health assistants, it is best when the primary caregiver role is shared by two people. Because of the demand on both time and emotions, it is too big a job for one person.

Dr. James Braun feels that the caregivers who have done the best are those whose lives are not exclusively centered around the relationship with the PWA. They value the person and their responsibility to him, but see it in a greater context or world view. The relationship with the PWA is seen as part of an overall approach to life, every aspect of which has meaning.

Being in the decision-making role for a person with AIDS may cause anxieties and uncertainty. For example, what is an emergency? When should we go to the hospital? When should I call the doctor? Does it help him to bring him this cup of tea, or should he get it himself? The patient's physicians and health care personnel can often help you answer these questions.

I once picked up a friend from the hospital after he had been there for an overnight blood transfusion. He was rolled to the door of the hospital in a wheelchair and then painstakingly limped to the curb and got into a cab. He winced with pain as the car stopped, started or hit a bump. As soon as he got to his apartment, he crawled into bed and wrapped himself in several blankets—on a 70 degree day. I learned later that day that his friends wanted to take him to Carnegie Hall for a concert that night. I thought the plan was irresponsible, almost cruel to think that he could endure the travel and sitting. I was shocked to find out a few days later that he had in fact gone to the concert and all had gone well. This event showed me that it is very hard to gauge someone else's capacity. One's ability can fluctuate dramatically in the course of a day.

It is hard to know what activity level would be most health-promoting. Another friend sold his business as well as his car and moved in with his mother after learning that he had some mild ARC symptoms. I encouraged him to make efforts to go out and do more. His mother told me after his death that he had truly been incapacitated by his illness, even during those early days, and simply was not capable of maintaining an activity level anywhere near what it had been in the past.

So many people with AIDS are caught in the middle. One friend will say they have to take AZT; another says take Dextran Sulfate; another will say they have to go to a healing circle; yet another will recommend changing doctors. The impact of all this is to put unnecessary pressure on the person with AIDS—making him think that if he fiddles with the combination lock a little more, the safe will open and health will be completely restored.

When you think of the person with AIDS, consider what attitudes you have, what you think the person needs. For example: Do you want him to get in touch with his feelings? Do you think he needs to return to work or quit his job? Do you want to prove how wise you are? Do you want to help him reestablish his relationship with God? Do you feel paralyzed by a sense of helplessness? Any of these points of view would interfere with your ability to simply sit and be with the person. I recently attended a memorial dinner for a man who had died of AIDS. A number of the guests commented at the dinner about how they thought his lover, Peter, was doing at grieving. Peter sensed that he was being judged by these guests and was hurt by that. Particularly at times which are so painful, people need love and support, not psychological assessments.

When asked how people can get their ill loved ones out

of denial, Stephen Levine replies: "Why would you want to get them out of denial? Why would you take away their dignity?"[3] You can not live someone's life and you cannot die their death. I have heard denial defined as our own mechanism for terror management. People gauge their ability to face AIDS and set the process at their own pace. Rather than trying to get the patient to see things differently, set an example by being in touch with your own pain. In that way you will demonstrate an ability to understand another's suffering. Jean Vanier, a Catholic priest, who has set up residences for the poor, the elderly and the handicapped, wrote, "Wounded people have taught me that I must learn to accept my weakness and not pretend to be strong and capable."[4] The emptiness of pretense becomes glaringly obvious when you are with a person who is dying. All the books about caring for the terminally ill which I have read stress that any falseness or "us/them" barriers, any subtle manipulations, all interfere with the healing that a human relationship can offer.

Let go of your expectation of being appreciated by the person with AIDS. He may express his gratitude, but probably will not. The person with AIDS might be angry, confused, easily frustrated. A tap on the feet intended as a gesture of affection may cause pain for the patient. Try not to let your frustrations or feeling unappreciated interfere with providing compassionate care. A support group would provide an opportunity to get perspective on your situation. One group of mothers of PWAs warns new group members to expect their sons to complain about their cooking, regardless of whether they praised it in the past.

Many people feel helpless and unsure of themselves when they visit their friend with AIDS at the hospital or at his home. Approach the situation assuming your importance to the patient while at the same time accepting your helplessness. In a world where people run from themselves and from each other, it is easy to forget that listening is a gift. Truth is often expressed and understood by silence. It is a great gift to hear the dreams and fears and memories of another person without wanting to add anything.

Ideally, the basis of your interaction is empathy. An empathic way of being means entering the private world of the other person and becoming thoroughly at home in that world. It requires you to put aside your own views and values.[5] Psychiatrist Leston Havens says "the conditions of empathy are the power to imagine the experience of another and then to express it."[6] Neither the imagining nor the expressing are easy. When talking with a person with AIDS, try to ask open-ended questions which will elicit feelings. Often we reassure people before they get their feelings out. For example, saying, "Oh, you'll be home in no time," when they are voicing fears about dying, or "I'm sure you can lick it," when they are talking about their slim chance of survival, may leave the person feeling more isolated. People in therapy groups are often asked not to touch a person who is sharing painful feelings because the reassurance of being touched could serve to block the experience of feelings which had been contained for years. Do not protect people by being too quick with comfort and, in so doing, conspire in the avoidance of pain.

It is also important to not have preconceived notions about what someone needs to say. I recently learned of a woman in her 70's, a devout Catholic, who was close to her death from cancer. She had lived her whole life going to church regularly and observing all the church's guidelines. During the days prior to her death, she said that she doubted if anything happened after death. Fortunately, her daughter did not squelch these thoughts, but let her air them without being threatened by her seeming abrupt lack of faith.

Dr. Bernie Siegel says that the family members of terminally ill patients often give the message to the patient, "Don't go, don't go," when what the patient needs to hear is "I love you."[7] One man told me of being with his lover at the moment of death. His lover enjoyed macrobiotic food and this man brought him what proved to be his last macrobiotic meal, which he had pureed before coming to the hospital. On this day he told his friend that he loved him and was willing to release him. A few moments later the man died in his arms. One woman told me of being with her husband as he died. He had refused to have his wedding ring removed at any time throughout their marriage—even, on two occasions, in spite of surgeons' requests prior to an operation. His fingers had become very thin; she decided that it was time to remove his ring. She started to pull the ring off his finger, but as she did so, his hand and arm began to tremble. She slid the ring back in place and his hand rested once again. "Then I realized that at some level he was hearing me. I sat with him that night and sang him songs which we had known and loved through the years."

I remember telling Swami Satchidananda that I was having difficulty conveying to others that they were in essence spiritual beings. Swami Satchidananda said the difficulty was due to the fact that I had not yet fully experienced my own spiritual awareness. We can not give something that we do not have. Your tools in helping someone with AIDS are your love and your commitment. The care is expressed in actions and words, as well as through silence. As you approach a person with AIDS, you offer yourself, including your frailties.

Family members should know that the person who is sick may spend more and more time sleeping and may at times be difficult to arouse. They will have a decreased need for food and drink. They may be confused about time, space and identity. They may become restless and do repetitive things such as pull bed linens. Try not to restrain these motions. Because of oral secretions, they may have difficulty breathing. Elevating the upper body with pillows can make breathing easier. Often the feet of people with AIDS are very sensitive to the touch. Ask if your touch is a comfort. It may be painful. Further ideas about how to approach the final days of life are discussed in the previous chapter.

Afterwards

Regardless of your faith, there is a period of feeling stunned after the death of a loved one. You may have thought you were prepared for the person to die, only to realize that it is almost impossible to be wholly prepared. You may be walking around the house waiting for the phone to ring, seeing the person's face in the faces of others, recalling memories which you may have thought were long forgotten. As one person said, "When I went shopping, it was for him. When I read the paper, it was for something to please both of us. Suddenly, none of it makes any difference."

The stages of the grief process (denial, anger, bargaining, depression, acceptance) outlined by Kubler-Ross do not occur over any fixed amount of time or necessarily in a definite sequence. Many people have seen one friend die of AIDS immediately after another, while at the same time facing their own HIV-related problems. This obviously complicates the grief process. You need regular opportunities to express your feelings in order to avoid living in a permanent state of emotional anaesthesia.

Plans for a funeral or memorial service are best made in advance. By planning ahead, the service can be designed to capture the spirit or uniqueness of the person who has passed away. A good example was the memorial service for Michael Hirsch, a friend and dynamic AIDS community organizer in New York City. The service included twelve eulogies by people Michael had chosen, a slide show, and a farewell visualization. Michael's preparation and the eloquence of all who participated enabled me—and, I would expect, many others—to leave the church with a feeling of knowing Michael better and being at peace with his life and death.

Ideally, the service will offer prayers for the soul of the departed, comfort for the loved ones, and serve as a way of recalling the deceased's life in a way which is loving and truthful. The dying process can pull together the different parts of a person's life. Often, in the case of a gay person with AIDS, there is the biological family and the family in the gay community. These two groups may be unfamiliar with each other and may have totally different perspectives on the person and ideas about how to honor the person's life in a memorial service. In some instances the lover of the person with AIDS, after having cared for him for many arduous months, has not been welcome at the service. The dying person should designate someone to be in charge of making plans who will accommodate the needs of the different segments of the person's life.

In the Orthodox Jewish tradition, sons say a daily prayer for one year after the death of a parent. This prayer glorifies God and does not focus on loss. You can adopt your own ritual—lighting a candle by a picture, saying a prayer by a particular tree, thinking of a way to honor the person in a manner which is appropriate for both you and your loved one. These remembrances are opportunities to honor your loved one and deepen your awareness of life.

Some time after the loss, it may be useful to channel your feelings into some form of service to others. A New York City group of mothers of PWAs arranged to offer their homes to the parents of other PWAs when they came to New York to visit their sons. Many of the hosting parents had already lost their sons to AIDS. This program is an excellent example of putting your personal grief into useful action and, in so doing, giving some meaning to a painful experience.

Part II

Learning from Others

❖

"Everything can be taken from a man but one thing: the last of the human freedoms—to choose one's attitude in any set of circumstances, to choose one's own way,"[1] wrote Viktor Frankl, a psychiatrist and Nazi concentration camp survivor.

In Part II we will look at people for whom AIDS or another seeming adversity was approached as an opportunity. When this idea was introduced at a recent seminar, one man asked, "AIDS is an opportunity for what?" John, a PWA, responded, "If it wasn't for AIDS I'd still be running around wondering what's the meaning of life but not bothering to find out. In the last year I've made strides that I hadn't made in 39 years. In that way, AIDS has been a great opportunity for self-awareness, an opportunity to heal my life."

The people we will learn from did not accept AIDS as an automatic death sentence. Their stories are inspiring and can help you choose a path which is self-empowering and health promoting.

Four

Facing the Challenge

❖

Your attitude towards AIDS may well reflect your attitude towards life. For example, a detached intellectual may approach AIDS with an aloof, analytical distance. Those who tend to be alarmists will run from pillar to post with the latest horror story; and people who bury their heads in the sand will do that with AIDS. Paranoid people might blame CIA germ warfare. The guilt-ridden blame themselves, while the excessively anxious make appointments with doctor after doctor. But AIDS is about life and death. To face AIDS effectively, more is required than our automatic psychological reflexes.

Let us begin by looking at our thoughts and feelings about AIDS. Please consider these questions: When did I first learn about AIDS? Why do I believe it is here? How have my concerns about AIDS changed over the years? How do particular people and information sources influence my feelings about AIDS? Can a person with AIDS do anything to affect the course of the illness? Is there anything I can do while the scientists seek their solution? How do I think it will end?

If your stance towards AIDS is a powerless one ("Why bother? We're doomed."), from the outset you face the challenge with an attitude which is physically and psychologically debilitating. All the ideas that follow in this book are of little value if you see no reason to face the personal and social challenges which AIDS presents. Viktor Frankl reports that shock, the first phase of the prisoner's psychological reactions upon admission to the death camp, preceded apathy. Although he acknowledges that apathy is a necessary psychological defense, Frankl states, "Woe to him who saw no more sense in his life, no aim, no purpose and therefore no point in carrying on. He was soon lost."[1] Psychiatrist Joel Dimsdale studied holocaust survivors and reached the same conclusion. Dimsdale pointed to several effective coping strategies: focusing one's attention on whatever good experiences occurred, having a group affiliation, observing Jewish holidays, resolving to survive for a special purpose. According to Dimsdale, every survivor testified that what kept him or her alive was "blind, naked hope."[2]

Apathy can follow the initial shock of receiving an AIDS diagnosis. Dr. Harold Kooden, a psychologist with extensive experience with the gay community, feels that a strong sense of one's future—a reason to be alive—is essential for surviving the health crisis. It is easy to look at the past with anger, at the government for doing so little, or at community leaders for failing to take action as the extent of the health crisis became evident; but our emphasis needs to be on what is to be done now.

Stephen Levine suggests making two lists. In the left column write why you wish to stay alive. In the right column, list why receiving a terminal prognosis may have caused some relief. Other authors who have written about their work with life-threatening illnesses recommend this or a similar technique. Levine stresses the need to examine that part of ourselves which for whatever reason may prefer death. "Looking directly into the boredom and self-doubt, the confusion and intense inner judgement, we see that during these states the mind often wishes not to be."[3] Thoughts and feelings cannot change until they are identified—not judged, but noticed and accepted. As Dr. R. Naomi Remen, Medical Director of Commonweal Cancer Help Program, says: "Without acceptance there is no way to take charge of your life. Without acceptance you just react out of fear. If you accept even the fact of death, then you can use it to tell you what's important—to cut through the bull, to love better."[4]

For one man, the self-generated healing process began when he admitted his feelings of hopelessness. For years Ed had been overinvolved in and overwhelmed by work. He found little joy in life and avoided closeness with others. One month after receiving an AIDS diagnosis, he said:

> I don't think I want to live. AIDS is an acceptable alternative to what is going on in my life. As a result I don't have a real will to do things that would promote my health. There's nothing that I want to do, no burning desires. No great interests, people to know, or places to see. I don't feel connected to anything.

I suspect that a great many people who are facing AIDS can identify with the sentiments Ed expressed. Ed said he was not motivated to become a long-term AIDS survivor. "Three years is not a long time. The virus runs its course no matter what you do." I did not challenge Ed on those points but sought another way of establishing an alliance with him. He said he did care about the quality of his life. He said he wanted to live with an awareness of what he was feeling, at peace with himself, and able to give and receive love. For Ed, the self-generated healing process began when he acknowledged that his goal was to improve the quality of his life on a one day at a time basis. Because he was able to tell others how he felt, Ed is making use of community programs, spiritually-based AIDS seminars, psychotherapy and friendships, all of which help him face having AIDS rather than give up.

The Chinese symbol for crisis also represents opportunity. Frankl acknowledges that those who choose to see the opportunity are few in number. Dr. Bernie Siegel estimates that fifteen to twenty percent of his patients see a cancer diagnosis as a challenge.[5] People with AIDS may have more possibilities than they realize, but they can not explore new possibilities until they have identified ways in which their beliefs may be limiting them.

In pointing out that twenty percent of PWAs have survived at least three years after diagnosis, Michael Callen, himself a PWA diagnosed in 1982, states: "The uncritical repetition of the myth that everyone dies from AIDS denies the reality of—but perhaps more important, the possibility of—our survival."[6]

Callen interviewed eighteen long-term survivors of AIDS. He reports that *every* one of the eighteen feels that their staying alive is related to their belief that survival is possible.

> If I had to describe in one word the common characteristic of the PWAs I interviewed, it would be grit. These people are all fighters: opinionated, incredibly knowledgeable about AIDS, stubborn, and passionately committed to living, they work hard to stay alive.
>
> Believing that I could survive is probably the precondition necessary for my survival. Unlike many other people with AIDS who considered themselves "ticking time bombs," my world view admitted from the first the possibility of recovery.[7]

Dr. O. Carl Simonton, a cancer specialist and pioneer in mind-body cancer work, was asked if his ideas could be applied to AIDS. "Yes," was his emphatic response; thoughts and emotions definitely influence AIDS. "How could it be otherwise?" he asked. "Look at the power our minds give to disease. They did it with leprosy, tuberculosis, then cancer, now AIDS. The power is in our minds, not in the disease."[8]

Tom tested positive to the HIV-antibody test one and one-half years ago. He believes he was exposed to the virus at least four but probably seven or eight years ago. He has had immune measures in blood work three times over the past 18 months. Although all three evaluations have reported immune levels in the normal range, the counts have improved each time. His advice to HIV-positive people:

> Simply lead a good, clean, healthy life. Don't get neurotic about being healthy. I went crazy over vitamins. They made me sick. I used to think that if I got emotional—depressed or angry—it could hurt my health. Then I convinced myself that I am healthy, no matter what, even if I get emotional. I convinced myself and reminded myself that I am healthy. If people stop being afraid, they at least have a chance. Giving up is the worst thing.

During a very moving talk with people with AIDS in New York City, Swami Satchidananda stressed the importance of hope:

> The first thought that I would like to share with you is never, never, never lose hope. The moment you lose hope you weaken the system a lot. A fearful person loses much of his stamina. That's why my advice is don't be afraid. Have that hope under any circumstances. That is the first way to block the drainage of the vital energy. By hope and courage we stop draining, but we can put back more also. That is where the natural disciplined life comes in. We call it yoga. Yoga is not something peculiar. It is just to lead a disciplined life, to do what is necessary to put back what is lost.

As he ended his talk, he emphasized the point again:

> Millions of people are thinking of you, praying for you. You're not alone in fighting this. But still, you have to do your part. I really wish you faith and strength and courage and hope. Let's march towards that and win the race. Thank you. And don't forget to laugh.

By reminding people to laugh, he was making the point that the "strict disciplined" life is also fun. He used two analogies to explain the healing process:

The real self is spirit, nobody can contaminate it, and nobody is doing anything with it. It is there, the pure self, like the sun. We say the sun is rising, the sun is setting. Is it true? The sun never rises and never sets. It's relative. From this side we say, "Yes, it's rising." We say the sun is giving us light. Go and ask the sun. It would say, "I don't know anything about giving or taking. I am just light. That's all I know. If you take light you say I am giving to you." If somebody closes his eyes, he says the sun is not giving me light. Should you blame the sun for it? No. Self is like that. Your pure Self is the pure spiritual energy, spirit. It is there, though it doesn't seem to do anything. If there's no sun, nothing happens in this world. Likewise, your Self is the inner sun. If we simply make ourselves clean, we'll be able to receive the energy.

To give another example: the music is here. Our mind and body is our radio. It should be tuned. Then you get the music. Unfortunately, our radios are completely out of alignment, out of tune, a lot of short circuits, a lot of loose connections, burnt out valves. How can we receive any music? Repair it. And if we tune it wrongly, there will be nothing but atmospheric disturbances. That is what we call yoga. Tuning your mind/body to receive the cosmic energy or nature's energy or God's energy, whatever you want to call it. It is there, available. It doesn't separate people. It is there everywhere. Those who tune receive it. The tuning is our part.

Much is required of the person who has chosen to see AIDS as an opportunity to maximize his or her emotional, spiritual and physical well-being. The first step is acceptance: acceptance that you, your child or lover or friend has AIDS; or that you have been told that you are HIV-positive. Acceptance is not easy and takes time. Our culture offers many means to avoid the pain in our lives—whether through the obvious routes of alcohol and drugs or the subtler paths of excessive work, shallow relationships, or the pursuit of money and glory.

Once a genuine acceptance has taken place, an openness follows. This has certainly been true in the varied approaches to treating AIDS. One PWA returned from an appointment with his rather traditional physician with the names of certain Chinese herbs which another patient of that doctor had taken with good results. Dr. Bernie Siegel tells of a man whose oncologist mocked his natural foods regimen cancer treatment. However, several years later when the oncologist learned that he had the same cancer, he promptly called his former patient to learn the specifics of this diet.

Another requirement is a steady and enduring determination. Often our best-intentioned exercise or weight loss plans rarely last more than a few days. With AIDS, what is required is learning to consistently view life in a hopeful, healthy manner. As Swami Satchidananda says, "The greatest and most difficult victory you can win is the victory over your own mind....These ideas seem to be very simple. Sometimes we don't seem to believe in simple things. We want a complicated approach because our life is complicated." It takes a gentle perseverance to gradually change the mental and behavioral patterns which interfere with our well-being. Many books on healing refer to the gradual process of deeply absorbing certain ideas—often a process that takes years.

Five

The Mind/Body Connection

❖

Recently there has been a resurgence of interest in the influence of thoughts, feelings, and life experiences on health. Although this belief in the mind's effect on the body extends throughout the history of medicine, its acceptance has varied according to the time. A new field of science called psychoneuroimmunology (PNI) studies the interrelationship of the mind (psyche), nervous system (neuro), and immune system (immunology). Many prominent hospitals now have body/mind clinics or staff trained in behavioral medicine techniques such as meditation, biofeedback, and autogenic training. These developments mark the beginning of a change in medical care in America. The emphasis during the past century had been on curing disease through identifying a microorganism of specific etiology. As Locke and Corrigan point out, this approach dominated medicine because it worked—leading to understanding and curing many diseases, among them tuberculosis, diphtheria, polio, and syphilis.[1]

However, the exclusive emphasis on treating disease by finding a microorganism can lead to the neglect of the role a person plays in coming down with a particular illness. That is, what is it about a person's life circumstances (e.g. at work, home, or within the person himself) that caused a specific disease at a certain time. These two perspectives are in evidence in the lifelong debate between Louis Pasteur and Claud Bernard, two prominent nineteenth century biologists. Pasteur believed that the seed (germ) was more important in understanding disease; Bernard emphasized the soil (body).[2] Finally, on his deathbed, Pasteur is said to have conceded that Bernard had been right.

People who are concerned about AIDS need to be concerned about both the soil and the seed. In the case of AIDS, the seed or germ is presumed to be the HIV virus. Therefore, one should be exceedingly careful to avoid exposure to this virus. Since sexual contact and IV drug use are the main routes of infection, the safest way to avoid HIV infection is not to shoot drugs and not have sex with HIV-infected people. If you are unsure of the HIV status of either yourself or your sexual partner, safer sex provides increased protection against HIV infection. Amidst the current emphasis on HIV, it is easy to overlook the health risks of other "germs"—for example, herpes viruses, Epstein-Barr virus, cytomegalovirus, parasites and amoebas, as well as syphilis, gonorrhea, and chlamydia. Scientists are in the process of learning about their long-term synergistic effects. Knowledge about your own health as well as that of any prospective sexual partner is essential in order to avoid unwanted difficulties.

But what about the soil? People who have AIDS, ARC, who are HIV-positive, or are at risk for being HIV-positive need to do all that is possible to bring optimum functioning to what Claud Bernard called the *milieu interieur* of the human body.[3] Those who live in a manner which naturally strengthens immunity do much better than those who passively submit to what they see as a likely death sentence.

The prevailing explanation of the course of HIV infection to full-blown AIDS is that the virus enters the body; lies dormant for a period of time, and then attacks the T4 cells—cells which initiate the body's attack against antigens (markers on infected cells); and, in so doing, leaves the body vulnerable to a series of opportunistic infections. Much of the scientific research on AIDS concerns how to prevent the HIV virus from doing its damage. However, from the vantage point of the soil, two other questions should be considered: Why do some HIV-positive people remain asymptomatic much longer than others? Can an individual do anything to increase this amount of time?

Dr. Anthony Fauci, the Director of the Office of AIDS Research for the National Institute of Health, reports that 30% of HIV-positive people develop full-blown AIDS within five years of infection; 50% have AIDS after seven years. Furthermore, Fauci reports that 90% show some signs of deterioration of the immune system within five years. It is not known whether those who have shown limited immune problems will eventually develop AIDS. No one knows exactly why some HIV-positive people develop AIDS and others do not. Dr. Fauci states that in order to maintain optimum health, "a good holistic approach together with therapy is recommended very strongly." He recommends good nutrition, reducing stress, and maintaining a positive attitude, as well as avoiding any noxious stimuli.[4]

The task for the HIV-positive or immune compromised person is to keep the soil as healthy as possible. HIV-positive people need to take initiative in seeing that they receive health care which itself is not immuno-suppressive and is consistent with the findings of psychoneuroimmunology. Many of the recent changes in health care in America have been initiated by the consumer. The women's movement has brought about changes in gynecological and obstetric care. Babies are now born by natural childbirth in birthing centers rather than with an anaesthetized mother and absent father. The hospice movement has enabled people to die peacefully in the company of loved ones. The women's movement did not wait for the American Medical Association to propose the idea of natural childbirth. Hospitals built birthing centers when they feared they would lose money by not having them. If you are at risk for AIDS, you need to educate yourself about signs of immune suppression and treatment possibilities. Don't count on anyone else to do this work for you.

Characteristics of Long-Term Survivors of AIDS and Other Illnesses

Studies are now being conducted with people who have survived AIDS for a minimum of three years. Johns Hopkins Medical Center and the Centers for Disease Control are conducting research into characteristics of long-term survivors. Unfortunately, many of the final results of these studies are not yet published. A preliminary report in *The Washington Post* (2/8/88) states that long-term survivors vary in terms of treatment, but they share a "fierce determination to survive" and have made an "uneasy peace with uncertainty and anxiety." After his interviews with long-term AIDS survivors, Callen concluded: "The psychoneuroimmunologists could be right; there may well be a will to live. Marshalling this will requires hope."[5]

At the American Psychological Association convention in August, 1989, recent research in psychoneuroimmunology was presented. Dr. Sandra Levy reviewed studies on psychosocial factors in disease outcome. She reported that the following interventions have been associated with improved immune function: group therapy, self-hypnosis, relaxation training, and cognitive behavior therapy. Dr. James Pennebaker's studies have shown that writing about traumatic experiences was associated with improved immune measures in undergraduates. Dr. Michael Antoni reports his findings that imagery, cognitive behavioral therapy, relaxation training, and social support enrichment were associated with increases in T4 cells and improved T4:T8 ratios in asymptomatic HIV-seropositive men. Dr. Levy concluded that scientists are on the verge of producing the one study that "pulls all the pieces together" concerning how psychosocial factors influence disease outcome.

Dr. George Solomon and his colleagues at the University of California at San Francisco offered the following profile of long-term AIDS survivors: They

(1) Accept the reality of an AIDS diagnosis, but refuse to believe that AIDS is necessarily an automatic death sentence;
(2) Refuse to be helpless or hopeless;
(3) Make lifestyle adjustments;
(4) Actively participate in a healing partnership with their health-care providers and take responsibility for their own healing;
(5) Share a powerful belief that life is worth living;
(6) Often have a previous history of overcoming obstacles;
(7) Value exercise and general fitness;
(8) Find value in peer support groups and in helping others;
(9) Are assertive and able to say "no";
(10) Are self-concerned and self-involved without being selfish;
(11) Are sensitive to the signals their body gives; and
(12) Are expressive and good communicators.[6]

Psychologist Lydia Temoshock, of the University of California in San Francisco, studied eighteen men with AIDS and found that men who were self-assertive had stronger immune systems than those who were more passive and nonexpressive.[7] Psychologist Carrie Milton studied 100 asymptomatic HIV-positive men. She found that those with strong commitments and a willingness to face challenges had greater numbers of certain immune-system cells.[8]

Niro Asistent's personal experience provides further testimony to the body-mind-spirit connection. She learned in November 1985 that she had ARC. This news came as her former lover's AIDS condition was worsening. She had night sweats, diarrhea, thrush, and tested HIV-positive. Believing that she had eighteen months to live, she decided to live out her life exactly as she had wanted to for many years—

meditating frequently, eating well, going for long walks on the beach. At a November, 1988 talk at the Integral Yoga Institute, Niro recounted her experience:

> I was diagnosed with ARC three years ago. I was very well educated by the media and I knew what that meant—that meant 18 months to live. I went through a whole realm of emotions. But one thing happened, I totally accepted that I had 18 months to live. I didn't doubt that. I know now that that was my wake-up call. I realized my days were counted. True, they were always counted. But suddenly I became conscious of it. And I chose to live my life differently. And very quickly I started to drop the bullshit. And my life was quite full of it. My life became very, very simple. I became very choosy about what I was doing every day. I became very selfish in a way. I did exactly what I wanted to do—not what society wanted me to do, not what my kids wanted me to do, or my parents, or my friends. For a while it was an uncomfortable time because guilt was there. It was hard to start operating that way. In our society it's not encouraged to live like that....
>
> What I did also—and that was really my tool for not going cuckoo—was to meditate every day. I had been a seeker all my life and I had led many meditation groups. So I knew I had the tool for not going crazy.... Now when I received the diagnosis, I promise you my tools went through the window. I forgot them all. I was totally lost. Little bit by little bit it came back. And I chose to meditate every day because that was the only moment when I was grounded in the day, when my mind finally could quiet a little bit. Otherwise, I was worried a lot, like many of you probably are if you are challenged by a condition like AIDS. As I meditated more and more, I was reaching other levels of consciousness

within myself. I was finding answers that I was always waiting for. What became my way of living was to live in the moment. So when I was washing the dishes, I was washing the dishes. When I was baking muffins, I was baking muffins. When I was watering the plants, I was watering the plants. It is something my teacher always told me, to live in the moment. I didn't know what he meant. And I really needed to force myself to do that. It's not something that came like that. I chose to do that because if I didn't do that I would go into: "What is going to happen to my kids? What is going to happen to my body? What if pain takes over? What if I'm in bed and I become dependent? People will need to wash me and bring me the pan." That goes with a lot of terror and hopelessness. I did not want to live the few days I had to live with that energy because it was taking the future into the present. I knew enough to realize that was totally ridiculous. That much I figured out....

So that's the way I started to live my life. *Moment by moment*....My body consequently started to improve. Night sweats started to disappear. Thrush started to disappear. Diarrhea definitely started to disappear. So somehow I knew I was on the right track—but not on the right track towards healing. I never sought that. I was on the right track to realize myself. Because that was much more important to me. I knew I was gonna die. I really wanted to die consciously this time. I still do. I knew that the quality of how I was living was something that I was looking for, I was longing for.

Then, one day—and for me it is an experience that is simple and difficult to explain—I had what is called a mini-satori or whatever—a moment of unity with the universe. I was walking on the beach. It was a special day. I was doing a meditation called vipassana, which is really walking consciously—where you walk very slowly with your hands in a receiving position and really being aware of where you put your heels and the rest of your feet, where your legs move. Being totally in the moment in watching that. I had a spiritual master. I always put him very, very high up there. And I was very eager to be a good disciple. That was taking a lot of my time and my thoughts and my energy. And suddenly I saw him in front of me. And instead of him being high up there, he just came down and we merged. Suddenly we were at the same level. I didn't realize totally the impact of that, but what it was was finally accepting the master within myself. I realized that the answer or whatever wasn't out there. It was really within. At that moment I knew I was fine. It was a moment of total acceptance. Again, the idea of not dying from the disease was not in my consciousness. But I knew I was fine. I knew something totally aligned within myself. And all of that might sound very metaphysical to you, but that's what happened to me.

It took another six weeks for me to go and get tested again. I knew something had changed. And when I went to the nurse, my counselor, I said, "You know, Jane, I'm fine." And the poor woman looked at me and said to herself, "She's a lunatic." She shared that with me afterwards. She didn't know what to do with me. I understand because in 1986 nobody was turning that kind of thing around. My test came back negative. They started testing my blood to find out what I did. Besides testing my blood, they didn't ask me anything else. And that created a kind of sadness to me. Because right away what I said to them was that I know that what I did, many people can do. I'm no different. The medical

> community, unfortunately, didn't really use me. I made myself totally available, but they didn't want to use me. Healing can happen on many different levels, many different planes. Not only on the physical. I know that my physical healing is the product of an alignment between the spiritual, the mental, and the emotional.

Niro has had no subsequent health problems. She has set up a program, SHARE (Self-Healing AIDS-Related Experiment), in which she helps others with their own healing.

At an October, 1988 seminar, Hal talked about his first AIDS hospitalization in December, 1981. "A friend of mine came to visit me. He had a seed catalogue, and we started planning a garden. It got me thinking about the future. The doctors were wondering if I would leave the hospital alive. Then I remembered hearing that who you spent New Year's Eve with is who you'll spend the year with. I decided to get out of the hospital and be with friends on New Year's Eve. It was a smart decision." Hal stresses the importance of not "buying into the belief that AIDS is 100% fatal."

In 1976, Dr. B.J. Kennedy at the University of Minnesota Medical School studied twenty-two people who had survived supposedly incurable cancer for at least five years. He found that, after the initial shock, these people were determined to fight the cancer. They stressed the importance of knowing someone who had survived their type of cancer.[9]

In *Anatomy of an Illness*, Norman Cousins describes his six months at a tuberculosis sanitarium at age ten. He reports that the patients divided themselves into two groups: those who were optimistic versus those who had resigned themselves to the worst. Cousins writes that he and other optimistic patients would do their best to recruit new admissions before "the bleak brigade went to work... I couldn't help being impressed with the fact that the boys in my group had a far higher percentage of 'discharged as cured' outcomes than the kids in the other group."[10]

❖

A review of research in psychoneuroimmunology points to several psychosocial factors which influence health. They will be presented in a group of five factors which strengthen immunity and three which weaken it.

What Strengthens Immunity

Faith and Hope

Peper and Pelletier conducted a computer search of "spontaneous remissions" from cancer. Spontaneous remission refers to the disease leaving the body without medical intervention. They found over 400 cases. No doubt thousands of others also experienced healing but did not return to the medical center to have a paper written about them.[11] Elmer and Alice Green studied these 400 cases and found that the most common factor was "a change of attitude prior to the remission—one which involved hope and positive feelings."[12]

The three reports that follow contain dramatic evidence of the power the mind has over the body. The common link in all three cases was the faith that healing was possible. It is not easy to remain hopeful amidst the deaths and frightening projections about AIDS, but the fact that some people who were terminally ill did beat the odds should provide hope for others.

Dr. Bruno Klopfer reported the famous case of Mr. Wright, a patient whose lymphoma was so advanced that death seemed imminent. An experimental cancer drug, Krebiozen, was being tested but the study was restricted to patients who were expected to have at least a few months of life remaining. Therefore, Mr. Wright was initially excluded from the study. After he pleaded for the drug, his doctor relented and included him in the three times per week injection schedule. When Dr. Klopfer returned to the hospital on a Monday after having administered the first injection the preceding Friday, he was startled to find Mr. Wright out of bed and conversing with patients and staff. His tumors had "melted like snowballs," and he was discharged from the hospital ten days after the first injection. Mr. Wright enjoyed two months of relative good health, until, upon reading reports that Krebiozen was ineffectual, he relapsed to his original state and was re-admitted to the hospital. Dr. Klopfer told Mr. Wright that he would be administering a double dosage of a new improved Krebiozen. In fact, Mr. Wright was placed in a control group and was given injections of sterile water. Again, he made dramatic improvement. The tumors shrunk and the fluid in his chest disappeared. He returned home, but, after a second two month period, Mr. Wright learned that the American Medical Association had concluded that Krebiozen was ineffective in cancer treatment. Mr. Wright became very sick, was re-admitted to the hospital, and died a few days later. His doctor reported, "His faith was now gone, his last hope vanished, and he succumbed in less than two days."[13]

Locke and Corrigan report a German doctor's experiment with three bedridden women, all of whom were not responding to conventional therapy. One had an inflamed gallbladder and chronic gallstones. Another was not recovering from abdominal surgery and had lost thirty pounds. The third was dying of cancer of the uterus that had metastasized. The doctor decided to try faith healing and contacted a local healer, who claimed to be able to heal without being in the physical presence of the patient. As arranged, he projected his healing powers to the three patients on twelve different occasions. No progress was made by any of the three patients. Then the doctor spoke to each patient—telling them of this healer and his many successes. He told them that the healer would be sending his healing force to them on a certain day. In fact, the healer did nothing on that day or subsequent days. However, each of the patients began a recovery process on the day that followed the supposed healing session. The woman with gallstones had no gallbladder problems for ten years. The woman who had lost so much weight following abdominal surgery regained the weight and recovered. The third woman's cancer had advanced to a lethal stage but the symptoms that had made her life unmanageable receded. She returned home and spent her final months without severe pain.[14]

The parents of Garrett Porter, a young man who at age nine was diagnosed with an inoperable brain tumor, were told by his doctors that he had less than a year to live. Garrett worked with a therapist and began a program of biofeedback and visualization. Each night he would relax thoroughly and then picture spaceships coming in and chipping off pieces of Planet Meatball, his name for his brain tumor. "Every night I would come in and blow it away completely, and then I'd start over again each night." After some time, he reported that he could not see the tumor at all. Six months later, Garrett fell at school. Because he showed signs of a possible concussion, he was given a CAT scan. The result of the CAT scan was that not only had he not had a concussion but that the brain tumor was gone as well. Garrett is now eighteen and, with his therapist, has written a book about his experience.[15]

You might find it hard to be hopeful if you have seen someone die from AIDS or are experiencing difficulties with your own immune system. At times I have had difficulty reconciling my own feelings of despair with Swami Satchidananda's unwavering message of "never, never lose hope." I once asked him, "In light of all the grim predictions about AIDS, how is it possible to be hopeful? He responded, "You are accepting their thoughts, the grim predictions. If you really know that somebody is going to discourage you, don't even have any friendship, any relationship, any relation with the person." On another occasion, I asked him if the prayer of a person with AIDS should be for health or surrender to God's will. His reply, "Both."

In a talk to PWA's, he told a story from his own childhood in which he and a friend were caring for animals on a farm. The other boy had been bitten by a snake and, with his hand bleeding, searched for half an hour through a pile of stones trying to find and then kill the snake. When the man in charge of the farm saw what the boy was doing, he said, "People die when they are bitten by a snake. You have to go do something, take some treatment." Swamiji recalled, "Immediately the boy fainted, not even a minute later. We had to carry him. It turned out that it was a non-poisonous snake, but the mere hearing about a poisonous snake bite was enough to make him faint." Swamiji went on to say, "That day showed me what suggestion can do. It's good to know the power of suggestion, the power of faith. Simply say 'No, I'm not going to die. I'm just going to get out of it. I will rebuild. I have the strength, and I have the know how. I will do it.' That kind of will is a great remedy that you can't get from any doctor. You have to develop it yourself."

But *AIDS?* Most scientists say it is 100% fatal. Ram Dass, a prominent American spiritual teacher, recently said that it can be cruel to give hope to people with AIDS. He acknowledged that hopelessness is harmful to both body and mind, then added, "There is something between hope and hopelessness—like 'Don't know.'" He teaches people to find an experience in themselves which is beyond a fearful mind. In the state of "Don't know," people accept that life is impermanent, and as Niro did, find comfort in the silence of each moment. As Michael Callen said, long-term survivors all remained open to the possibility that survival from AIDS is possible. For Swami Satchidananda, hope includes resolute determination. For others—Niro Asistent, Ram Dass—it involves a continual resolve to be open to whatever happens in each moment, as you live in a way that maximizes health. Neither approach advocates hopelessness; rather, there is a difference in emphasis.

I have seen people whose professed hopefulness about AIDS seemed false. They were trying to convince me so that they could convince themselves. That is not the hopefulness that heals. The hopefulness that promotes health comes from an attitude of *living with AIDS*—not running from AIDS.

A Sense of Purpose in Life which Includes a Bold, Defiant Attitude toward the Illness

Ikemi and his colleagues at the Kyushu University School of Medicine in Japan report the case of a man who first had cancer of the jaw. The cancerous growth was removed surgically. The same patient returned a few months later and learned that he had cancer of the vocal chord. Surgery was recommended but the patient refused it—saying that his voice was needed for his preaching at church. He also refused radiation therapy and chemotherapy. "This is God's will. Whatever should happen, will happen." Years later an amazed doctor reported, "The patient seems dramatically cured. The tumor was gone." The patient died of a back injury thirteen years after the vocal chord cancer diagnosis.[16]

The patient's response to having cancer of the vocal chord reflects the bold faith which is often found in cancer survivors. Norman Cousins reports his conversation with a group of cancer patients who had lived past their doctors' predictions. One patient's explanation of her survival was that when her doctor "gave me a few months to live" she looked at him and said, "Go f— yourself".[17]

A group of London researchers under Keith Pettingale reported that 75 percent of those who had a "fighting spirit" in response to cancer diagnosis survived 10 years in contrast to a 22 percent survival rate in those who responded with a "stoic acceptance."[18] Research with breast cancer at the National Cancer Institute concluded that the survivors were "fighters". Dr. Sandra Levy followed a group of 36 women who had been diagnosed as having advanced breast cancer. She concluded that a sense of joy in life was the psychological factor that mattered most for survival.[19] University of Iowa psychiatrist Dr. Ziad Kronfol has tested blood from clinically depressed patients and found that their immune systems are less responsive than those of normal individuals.[20]

These studies and case histories show how a positive attitude towards life as well as illness play an important role in promoting health. Albert Schweitzer "believed that the best medicine for any illness he might have was the knowledge that he had a job to do, plus a good sense of humor."[21]

However, the truth is that most people are not joyful and fearless about having AIDS or any other serious illness. Steven James makes the point that if you assert "I am going to heal myself" but subconsciously feels "No, I am going to die" the first statement has "little going for it other than a nice wish which might have a tranquilizing effect." He sees this alternative statement as having more truth and, therefore, more power: "I am *working* to heal myself. I don't know what the final outcome will be, but I'm sure going to do my best." What is necessary is that you be able to express whatever thoughts and feelings are being experienced.[22] Pennebaker reports that the stress of loss can be lessened by sharing your sorrow with someone else.[23] Siegel reports two additional studies which concern the importance of acknowledging and expressing feelings. In the first, undergraduates who recorded their feelings in a journal on a daily basis had stronger immune functions than those in the control group. In the second study, hospitalized patients seen by the head nurse as "bad" patients invariably had stronger immune systems than those designated as "good" patients. The explanation was that the "bad" patients were self-assertive rather than passive in their dealings with the nursing staff. Their requests for prompt care and explanations of treatment antagonized the nursing staff but served to promote their health.[24]

The people whose bold, defiant attitude toward their illness led to healing were in no way superficial in their conviction. Their sense of purpose in life was felt in their gut. By facing thoughts and feelings, and admitting fears to loved ones, you find an inner strength which fosters health.

Being True to Yourself

Lawrence LeShan, a scientist/therapist whose writings on meditation and the mind/body connection are well-known, reports that there are basically three reasons people give for not wanting to die: 1) fear of the circumstances of death—the pain, the unknown, the helplessness; 2) wanting to live for others, to fulfill their demands or expectations; or 3) wanting to live "to sing the unique song of one's own personality." LeShan says:

> For reasons I do not fully understand, the body will

> not mobilize its resources for either or both of the first two reasons. Only for the third will the self-healing and self-recuperative abilities of the individual come strongly into play. When individuals with cancer understand this and begin to search for and fight for their own special music in ways of being, relating, working, creating, they tend to begin to respond much more positively.[25]

There are a number of interesting studies and case histories which point out the benefits of living in a manner which is authentic for a particular person. Weiner reports the story of a man who, as a boy, wanted very much to become a violinist. However, his father forbid this, calling it too effeminate. The man became a banker and in his mid 50's learned that he was dying of "incurable" leukemia. He stopped banking, took up the violin, and the leukemia went into remission.[26]

Michael Marmot conducted research with Japanese immigrants in the San Francisco area. He found that those Japanese who retained their cultural roots had a lower incidence of heart disease and other illnesses. They differed from other Japanese citizens in America only in that they maintained their ties with Japan by socializing with other Japanese, speaking the language, observing the holidays, etc. Even if they adopted American habits (e.g. smoking, high fat food), they remained healthier than other Japanese-Americans. Breaking with one's tradition, according to Dr. Leonard Syme, can be hazardous to your health.[27]

Michael Lerner, quoting William Blake, believes that healing involves "unique particulars" for each individual. He told of one man, a retired pediatrician, whose healing process included caring for an abandoned cat. When Hal discusses his experiences with having AIDS over the past eight years, he frequently makes statements such as, "A little voice inside me said, No." Or, "I had a feeling in my gut to seek a certain treatment." Hal's language reveals his trust in his own inner wisdom.

"To thine own self be true" is not easy for gay people who feel the need to participate in society and to be close to their families of origin, but not at the cost of denying or concealing a major part of themselves. It is easy to feel alienated at a family gathering if you are unable to mention the people and feelings which are central in your daily life. Furthermore, certain aspects of the gay community have not provided the emotional and spiritual nurturance that people need. Create a life that is deeply satisfying—with fulfillment in your career, in your work place, in your social network, in your love life, and your inner life. It is worth taking time to consider the "unique particulars" of both your own healing process and your contribution to others during this epidemic.

Participation in the Healing Process

Jerome Frank, in *Persuasion and Healing*, studied cases of miraculous cures at Lourdes, a city in southern France known for its reported spiritual healings. Among the less than one hundred cases which met the criteria for miracle cure according to the standards of the Catholic Church, none lived near Lourdes—even though thousands of people from the area visited the shrine each year. Frank believes that the healings were in part the result of the pilgrimage itself. People travel to Lourdes from thousands of miles away. The preparation for the trip—including raising money, the farewell at one's home church, the emotional power of the travel itself, the reception by the volunteers at Lourdes, and the many group prayer sessions—all contribute to healing.[28]

Participation in the healing process refers to the patient's active role in his treatment. This involvement enhances health. Kavanagh compared severely burned children, who were taught to change their own dressings, with other children who received standard care. The children who dressed their own wounds needed less pain medication and had fewer complications. Similarly, Siegel reports that asthmatic children, who are taught about their disease and drugs used to control it, missed fewer days of school and had fewer emergency room visits.[29]

No one can accuse the gay community of failing to participate in its own healing process. People *are* involved—whether it be through volunteer work, participation in an alternative treatment experiment, attending a healing circle, or going to Washington to protest at the Food and Drug Administration. Many PWAs spend time each day reading about AIDS or attending lectures on new treatment possibilities. In fact, for some the problem is overinvolvement, running from lecture to lecture without stopping to formulate their own daily plan to promote health.

Loving Family and Friends

People do not live in isolation. We all need each other. Research has shown that health is promoted by a loving, social network. Lawrence LeShan found that many cancer patients had experienced loss of loved ones prior to their diagnosis.[30] Parkes studied widowers and found that they died at an unusually high rate within six months of their wife's death.[31] Schleifer noticed a decline in immune strength after the death of a spouse.[32] In a study of the Harvard Class of 1947, psychiatrist George Valliant reported that those who were satisfied with their lives had one-tenth the death rate of those seen to have the worst mental health.[33] Berkman's study in California found that those with a good social network had one-third the mortality rate of those who were isolated.[34] Psychologist Janice Kiecolt-Glaser found that those who were extremely lonely had immune systems with the greatest impairment.[35]

One seminar participant, a man diagnosed with AIDS two years ago, said, "For many years I chose destructive behaviors that were certainly connected with the lack of self-love. For me, what broke the cycle was getting close to another human being. I experienced intimacy and caring for the first time in my life.... It strengthened my self-love, and I started to make more choices which were pro-life rather than pro-death."

Many gay men have troubled relationships with their families. Either the family never recovered from the son's disclosure about his homosexuality, or the son chose to avoid the issue by never discussing his personal life when he was with his family. Obviously, this makes it all the more difficult to tell your parents that you have AIDS. PWAs need not choose isolation. Often love and comfort will appear when you least expect it.

What Weakens Immunity

In the preceding discussion of factors which strengthen immunity, some implications about what weakens immunity are self-evident. The research stressing the value of a loving social network points to the harmful effects of *loneliness* and *depression*. Much remains unknown about *how* the mind can weaken the immune response, but the fact that it does is undeniable. What follows is a discussion of three psychosocial factors — fear, helplessness, stress — which weaken immunity. When people learn about this, they sometimes become stressed about their stress or afraid of their own fears. People who are facing AIDS will experience fear and helplessness and stress. *What is harmful is when these emotions are suppressed or prolonged.* At one seminar, a man talked about being upset about his recent AIDS diagnosis. He was afraid that his depression would weaken his immune system still further. He was reassured when another group member said to him, "It would be a little strange if you weren't depressed at this time. I know I was."

Fear

Psychologist Robert Ader, a pioneer in the field of psychoneuroimmunology, conducted a famous experiment in which he used classical conditioning to induce nausea in rats. Classical conditioning is best known as the mechanism which Pavlov used to condition dogs to salivate at the sound of a bell. Ader injected rats with cyclophosphamide, a drug that induces nausea, and then immediately gave them saccharin-flavored water. One administration of cyclophosphamide with saccharin usually caused the rats to become nauseous when saccharin was subsequently given by itself. Ader was surprised to find that the rats in his study were dying. He later learned that cyclophosphamide was a powerful immunosuppressant! In other words, merely by drinking saccharin, the rats were conditioning themselves to weaken their immune system to the point of death. For these rats, the taste of sweet water had the immunosuppressant effect of cyclophosphamide. This study shocked skeptics but was replicated by other scientists who obtained the same results. While Ader's findings are not explicitly about fear, they do show that the immune system does not act independently of the brain. Prior to this study, scientists did not believe that immune functioning could be conditioned by the nervous system. Mental associations—however they are conditioned—can have a powerful effect on the body.[36]

Swami Satchidananda tells a story in which Yama, the God of Death, sent a messenger to a village to kill 500 people from cholera. As he returned from the town, an observer was furious because 2,000 had died. The emissary explained that, in fact cholera had killed 500, and fear had killed the other 1,500." "AIDS may kill a few people. But fear will kill thousands," says Satchidananda.

Our society encourages the illusion that sickness, old age, and death can be kept out of our lives. If you have AIDS, it becomes harder to pretend that you are indestructible. In order to face AIDS effectively it is necessary to look at your fears of life, your fears of intimacy, isolation and rejection, of defeat and humiliation, of vulnerability and weakness. Facing these fears becomes a vital dimension in your healing.

Helplessness

Psychologist Martin Seligman has spent many years conducting experiments which show that people often approach life assuming that they are helpless and unable to exert power over the events in their world. This helplessness—not the life events themselves—is what depletes immunity.[37] An experiment by psychologist Jay Weiss illustrates this point.

Weiss took pairs of rats and exposed them both to the

same stress—mild shock in the tail. However, one of the rats could rotate a wheel which could turn off the shock. The other rat had no means to discontinue the shock.[38] Both rats received the same number of shocks with the same intensity. However, the helpless rats developed ulcers twice as fast as those that could control the shock. Visintainer conducted a similar study in which rats were injected with live tumor cells. Cancer developed in 73% of the helpless rats, but in only 37% of the rats who could exercise control of the shock.[39] Seligman did a study in which dogs which had been taught to be helpless later lay down and exposed themselves to shock rather than go to a part of the cage in which no shock was being administered.[40]

During the 1960s, psychiatrist Peter Bourne did biochemical stress research at an American military camp near the Cambodian border. While Bourne was at the camp, the soldiers intercepted a radio message indicating that the Vietcong would attack the American base at some point between May 18 and 22—but most likely on May 19. Both the officers and enlisted men took action to prepare for the attack; Bourne found that stress levels were very similar for these two groups during the preparation period. The enlisted men laid out additional mines, reinforced barbed-wire defenses, prepared a bunker for the casualties. The officers were in constant radio contact with their headquarters. May 19 came and went; there was no attack on May 19 or on subsequent days. It was a false alarm. On the days of the expected attack, the officers had significantly higher stress levels than the enlisted men. Bourne's explanation of the difference in stress levels for two groups who faced an equally life-threatening situation was that the enlisted men could convert their anxiety into clear-cut action while the officers' responsibilities were more psychologically demanding and less defined. They had to worry about the base and how their performance would be evaluated by their superiors.[41]

Steve attends the seminars because his lover died of AIDS. He is not HIV-positive but has a serious heart problem which has caused him to be on disability for the past fifteen years. He had experienced extreme pain and feared living with chronic pain. He said:

> Ten years ago I spoke to doctors and found out what pills would be necessary to kill me from an overdose. I had been terrified about being in pain in the future. The very instant I got the pills a tremendous weight lifted off my shoulders. I knew that I would never be subjected to unending pain. My pain diminished as soon as I got the pills. It's ten years later. I'm still so grateful, knowing those pills are there. I don't think I would have lived if I hadn't done this.

For Steve, getting the pills was an act of self-control that removed his feelings of hopelessness. Having the pills has enabled him to live peacefully and without pain.

A person facing AIDS lives with a fearful uncertainty not unlike that of a soldier whose base could be attacked at any minute. What Bourne's study suggests is that anxiety becomes increasingly manageable when it is converted into constructive action. For the person with AIDS these actions can take various forms—for example, an exercise or nutrition program or participation in community meetings. Anxiety diminishes when you know that you are taking steps toward promoting well-being. Seligman contends that passive surrendering to life creates an emotional and behavioral pattern which is unhealthy physically and psychologically. Because the media often describes AIDS as "always fatal"—even though 15% of the people diagnosed five or more years ago are still alive—people with AIDS need to be on guard against feeling helpless.

Stress

Much research has been conducted concerning the role of stress on immune functioning. When it is used here, stress refers to the perception of individuals that their life circumstances have exceeded their capacity to cope. In this context, stress occurs within the person in his or her subjective experience.[42] The term stress was introduced by Hans Selye, an organic chemist, whose book, *The Stress of Life* remains a classic in the field. Selye observed a three-part physiological response to stress in animals: enlargement of the cerebral cortex; atrophy of the thymus, spleen, and lymph nodes; and deep bleeding stomach and duodenal ulcers.[43] Riley's 1981 research with rats concluded that the degree of stress, in this case rats continually revolving at 16, 33, 45, or 78 RPMs, directly correlated with the size of cancerous tumors that the rats had been bred to contract. Although the rats appeared to be adjusting to life on a turntable, subsequent analysis proved that the faster the rotation, the larger the tumor.[44]

Other research with stress confirms the studies about helplessness which conclude that it is not the stress itself that affects health as much as the individual's response to it. Metropolitan Life conducted an actuarial study of people in high level jobs in Fortune 500 companies. The researchers found that the mortality rate of these executives was approximately one third that of other white males of approximately the same age. Those with high ability to control their work are much healthier, even if they have very demanding jobs.[45]

The effect of expectations on life experiences was demonstrated in a study by Shlomo Breznitz, a psychologist at Hebrew University in Jerusalem. Breznitz told three groups of Israeli soldiers that they would be marching either 30, 40 or 60 kilometers. In fact, all three groups had to march 40 kilometers. Some groups were allowed to see distance markers; others were not. Stress levels reflected the soldiers' estimates of how far they had marched, rather than the actual distance. Those who were given accurate information showed lower stress measures.[46]

Hans Selye himself reports being diagnosed at age 65 with reticulum cell sarcoma, a cancer whose cure rate is extremely low. Selye realized he could be a "miserable candidate on death row" or "squeeze as much now from life as he can." He chose to cut down his stress level as much as possible. He reports, "Look what happened. I turned out to be the fortunate exception."[47]

Psychologist Joan Borysenko's personal response to a challenge demonstrates an effective coping strategy. After deciding to begin jogging, she convinced herself that she lacked the genetic make-up for such an arduous undertaking. One day she saw a television story about an older woman who had gradually built up to jogging 40 miles per week. Borysenko reports that she would say to herself, when jogging, on the inhalation "If she can do it," and, on the exhalation, "so can I."[48] After a few months she was jogging five miles at a stretch. A man at an AIDS Seminar told his personal experience with AIDS:

> I want to tell a story of too much acceptance and not enough stress. It depends on what we do with that stress. I was diagnosed with AIDS four years ago and was told I had no T cells in my body at all. I accepted what the doctor said to me—that once you get a T cell value below 100 you are pretty much gone. I told my boss I had to leave. I work in a very stressful job in advertising. There's nothing more stressful. I told them I was going to go away for a month and I was probably going to resign. I went away for a month. I stayed in a country house and got sicker and sicker. There was no stress, it was totally relaxing, and I still was accepting the fact that the doctor said that I don't have much time left. My boss finally got in touch with me and said, "This is ridiculous. Come back to work. We'll work something out." And here it is four years later and I still have almost no T cells. But I'm still here. I accept the fact that I have what I have. But I refuse to accept the fact that I'm going to die. I'm going to be here for 40 years. I don't care what anybody tells me. I still have all this stress, but I think I've learned how to throw that stress away. I go to the gym. Instead of getting on the bus or the train to go home after work, I walk home so I don't throw myself from one stressful environment to another. And I'll

relax on the way home and leave all that stress behind. I don't know what I'm doing but I now have 17 T cells. That's why I'm here. I want to tell people about the power of the mind. And it's so true. It works. It's real. Use it. Just bring it in and feel it in every part of your body. Feel the good stuff, not the bad stuff. Don't read the newspapers. Who needs to read the news and all this negativity. There's positive energy out there. Even in New York. It's here. Find it if you want it.

Six

Taking Charge of Our Lives

❖

People often feel overwhelmed and do not know how to begin the process of self-generated healing, also called self-induced healing or, simply, self-healing. "I'm *not* hopeful. I've seen people die and I think I'm next. What can I do about that?" "I saw a man waiting at the doctor's office. He looked wretched—like death. And you know what my first thought was. I don't want that to happen to me." "I know stress is harmful, but what can I do to reduce it?" These are the statements of those who are able to verbalize their concerns. For many, the fear and helplessness are so pervasive that the individual can not see the dilemma he or she is in. However, the very fact that people at risk for AIDS are attending a seminar or reading a book on living with HIV distinguishes them from others at risk. Michael Lerner has studied hundreds of alternative cancer centers and found that those who attend these centers are more educated and motivated than those who do not explore these possibilities.

This chapter is designed to help you evaluate how you are doing at applying the principles of self-generated healing. In Chapter Five we reviewed some of the research and case histories demonstrating the traits and behaviors that either enhance or impair health. Many other studies could have been presented which would have provided further evidence of the important role of thoughts, emotions, and life experiences on our physical well-being. Five factors were found which aid the healing process. They are: faith and hope; a sense of purpose in life which includes a bold, defiant attitude toward the illness; being true to yourself; participation in the healing process; loving family and friends. Fear, helplessness, and stress, on the other hand, hinder the healing process. Self-generated healing takes these ideas and puts them to work in daily life.

Let us start with an honest assessment of where you are now. The factors we will evaluate here are often measured by carefully designed psychological tests. Here you are asked to conduct a self-assessment and then discuss the results with two or three others—a lover, close friend, family member, therapist, or whoever knows you well.

Please respond to these questions by using a 0-10 scale. A score of ten represents a very well-established feeling that you possess the health-enhancing quality. A zero scores indicates not having that quality at all. Please answer these questions honestly—as you truly feel and not as you think you should respond.

Faith and Hope

1. Do I believe that survival is possible?
2. How much hope do I have that an individual can make himself a long-term AIDS survivor?
3. Do I believe that there is a force beyond my personal capacity which can help me through difficult times?
4. Do I believe that an individual's thoughts and feelings can promote the healing process?

Sense of Purpose in Life which Includes a Bold, Defiant Attitude toward the Illness

1. Do I have an ongoing sense that my life has a purpose (for example, a purpose experienced through personal challenges or responsibilities to others)?

2. Are there events in the future which I want to experience?
3. Do I have reasons for living?
4. Concerning AIDS, do I have a dynamic, fighting attitude?

Being True to Yourself

1. Do I have a sense of what makes me unique as a person?
2. Do I have particular interests which I pursue?
3. Do I live in a manner which I feel is being honest with how I want to live?
4. Am I able to express strong personal beliefs which others may not agree with?

Participation in the Healing Process

1. Are there daily activities which I do to promote my health (for example: exercise, meditation, following a particular diet)?
2. Do I make efforts to be knowledgeable about AIDS and various treatment options?
3. Am I actively rather than passively involved in the healing process?
4. Am I willing to do the work that self-generated healing requires?

Loving Family and Friends

1. Are there people in my life with whom I can freely express my feelings (love, anger, affection)?
2. Are their people who share their innermost concerns with me on a regular basis?
3. Are there people who need my love?
4. Are there people in my life who can help me with the tasks of daily living (shopping, laundry, errands, etc.)?

For the following three items, *high* scores indicate the *absence* of the health-impairing quality. For example, a relative *lack* of fear would be scored 8-10.

Fear

1. Am I able to keep my fears about AIDS under control?
2. To what degree am I able to live a worry-free life?
3. Can I keep myself from dwelling on the possibility of incapacitating illness or death?
4. Am I able to face and express my fears before they magnify to an unmanageable degree?

Helplessness

1. Do I see myself as a person who generates strategies to face challenges in life?
2. Do I feel that I can take constructive actions to face AIDS or do I feel helpless?
3. Do I keep myself from succumbing to a sense of powerlessness concerning AIDS?
4. When a problem with AIDS arises, do I strive to maintain a solution-oriented mentality?

Stress

1. Am I able to manage the stress of daily life?
2. Am I knowledgeable about techniques for dealing with stress? (deep relaxation, exercise, time management, self-assertion skills)
3. Do I use these skills on a daily basis?
4. Can I prevent my life (job, social life, home, etc.) from causing significant wear and tear on my body?

This informal assessment should help you gain a sense of where you stand in terms of having the traits and life circumstances which enhance the healing process. The numerical scores provide a means of comparison between the eight categories. Because we are all capable of self-deception, it is important to go over your responses to these questions with one or two trusted friends or family members. After honest discussion with these people, you should have a good sense of your present capacity for self-generated healing.

Each person's path to healing is unique and takes different shapes over time. If you have a deficit in one particular area—for example, you have loving family and friends, participate in the healing process, but lack faith and hope—then the hopelessness should be addressed. Anyone can follow the path of self-generated healing. What follows are suggestions for facing deficits in each of the eight areas discussed above.

Very often the example of others is beneficial in giving people faith and hope. This is a basic tenet of Alcoholics Anonymous and other self-help groups. It is not easy to be hopeful about having AIDS when you have no knowledge of others who have found meaning in the experience and learned ways to maximize their health. Read books and articles about healing and avoid reports which are discouraging. AIDS support groups need to avoid an "Ain't it awful" mentality. People who destroy your hope should also be avoided.

A sense of purpose in life is not easily taught. I recall reading a 17-year-old boy's poem about finding meaning in life. He weighed different means for fulfillment—fame, fortune, family, sexual conquests, professional accomplishments, spiritual realization. He was wondering which path or paths to follow. Many people do not take the time to consider this in their youth or adult life. They unconsciously live the life which their society and family steer them into. One way to find value in your life is by asking what has brought you contentment and fulfillment in the past—for example, moments of inner silence, accomplishments at work or school, experiences of love, appreciation of nature or art. How could these experiences occur in the future? Our experience is not what happens in our life but what our reaction is to it. Beauty, dignity, and purpose can be found in the most painful circumstances. The shamans did not see prolonging life as the most important goal of healing—rather it was to see that life was in balance, that the person was at peace with his or her soul, and that one's sense of personal power was restored.

Some people naturally seem to have a bold and defiant attitude toward their illness. Paul Tillich wondered if "thymos"—a Greek word which could be translated as the courage to be and is the root of thymus, a central gland in immune functioning—is a quality given to people in varying amounts.[1] You can learn to be courageous by beginning with small challenges and gradually building up to larger ones. The first step is the decision to face HIV rather than hide from it. Subsequent steps will present themselves on a daily basis.

It is not easy to be true to yourself. Going against a cultural norm can be painful—whether it be, for example, a teen-ager choosing music or clothes which are not popular with his peers; or deciding to keep a kosher diet in a secular world; or acknowledging one's sexual feelings in a culture hostile to divergent sexuality; or expressing one's spirituality in a community which does not understand the value of prayer and meditation. Being true to yourself does not mean an ostentatious imposition of yourself on others—rather, discerning how to live in a manner which is authentic and nurturing. People often bury their individuality with internalized messages from childhood. They believe they should not stand out or be proud of themselves. Again, in order to live a life which is consistent with your own uniqueness, begin on a one day at a time basis. Be aware of what you would enjoy doing today. Consider what particular gifts you have to offer others. What are your specific opportunities for learning, the challenges you are currently facing. There is a story about Rebbe Zusya, a mystic who lived in Central Europe during the 1700's. He attended the funeral of a man whose life was compared to the lives of great holy men. "He was like Moses, like David," the mourners said. After the service, Rebbe Zusya said, "At my funeral I hope they don't say I was another Abraham or Moses, but that I was a great Zusya."

Many people are passive about their health—seeing health as merely the absence of disease. Health is a far more dynamic and active state. Self-generated healing requires daily involvement. Adopt a plan that you *want* to pursue, set realistic goals for a limited time period, and then begin. What we are talking about is much more important than losing a few pounds. Don't make a plan that you can not or will not follow. I see yoga practices, careful nutrition, meditation, exercise, and social support as all being important in the healing process.

The final category for promoting health is loving family and friends. Some people may feel that there are people with whom they can freely give and receive love. Many others may feel lonely or dissatisfied with current relationships. Learning to love is a lifelong process and can not be taught in one paragraph. Nevertheless, you can think about your current relationships—in what ways they reflect your goals and aspirations, in what ways they are fulfilling, and in what ways they could be healed. If you feel that your life is without a person to share embraces, joys, and sorrows, ask yourself if you are honestly willing for someone to enter your life. There is no room for a lover when your mind is filled with fears, memories of failure, and emotional armor.

Overcoming fear is what prompts many pursuits, including spiritual journeys. Many statues of the Buddha show him seated with his hand raised in the "abhaya mudra"—meaning "Fear not." "Be not afraid" is a central teaching of Christianity. We fear death, we fear each other, and we fear our own thoughts and feelings. The fear of death and the fear of loss are deep within the mind. Running only magnifies our fear. This is expressed by a dream in which a man was being chased at night by a large ferocious dog. After running through abandoned city streets, the man turned and walked toward the dog. When he reached it, he found himself petting a gentle puppy. Our fears are like that. The fears people face with AIDS are not small ones—sickness, incapacitation, and death. But you can gain strength from others who have faced these fears and learned to be at peace with them. This comfort can come from talking with PWAs, reading about those who have had near-death experiences, and studying the teachings of those who have guided others in facing these fears honestly and thoroughly.

Helplessness is hazardous to your health. It is "characterized by a decreased motivation to do anything about life's difficulties and by a negative mind-set that makes it hard to appreciate that you did something right when you actually do change a situation," according to Borysenko.[2] Helplessness can be a character trait which is often established early in life and subsequently reinforced. Psychotherapy, reading, and support groups are all invaluable when you feel paralyzed in your efforts to face AIDS.

Stress can be reduced. By learning the techniques of stress management, you can dramatically reduce your level of stress within several weeks. Deep muscle relaxation can be learned from stress management workbooks or courses; relaxation audiotapes can be found in most bookstores. Diet and drug intake influence our state of well-being. The stimulant effect of caffeine can make relaxation very difficult. Excessive alcohol consumption is immunosuppressive and its depressant effect can diminish our commitment towards healing. Stress is often the result of a lack of self-assertion. Many people's lives are filled with tension because of failure to assert themselves at work or with friends and family. You can learn to be self-assertive. This does not mean being aggressive toward others but behaving in a manner which acknowledges the rights of all involved. Another cause for stress is not knowing how to manage time. If you have unrealistic goals for a day—for example, running ten errands when only three are possible—you will finish your day with a sense of frustration.

This chapter contains suggestions about how to develop the specific traits or life circumstances which enhance healing. It is hard work. The changes we are talking about are not superficial ones; hope and empowerment must reach down to your gut. I once heard a lecture in which the speaker asked an audience totally unfamiliar with opera, to sing the aria "Un Bel Di." No one knew the aria and, therefore, nobody sang. She explained that in order to teach us she would have to break the piece down and teach it to us bar by bar. The same is true with learning the process of self-generated healing. Set your goals and proceed step by step.

Part III

The Path of Self-generated Healing

❖

You have just seen how health is influenced by thoughts and emotions. The path of self-generated healing involves approaching life and illness in a manner which is based on faith, self-empowerment, and hope. But the path presented in this book also includes specific practices—each of which play a vital role in healing. These practices are: daily meditation; imagery exercises; Hatha yoga, including breathing practices; a whole foods diet; regular exercise; and keeping a daily journal. For now, the next step is to read these chapters and get a sense of what feels right for you. Try not to be overwhelmed. Part III ends with recommendations about how to establish your own plan for healing.

Seven

Meditation

❖

Meditation is not easy to write about because it involves experiences that are beyond thoughts or descriptions. Much of what will be discussed here is actually the preparation for meditation—a word used in this chapter to refer to conscious efforts to focus and then transcend the mind. Ordinarily we live with very little control or perspective on the activity of our minds.

There are a wide range of approaches to meditation, leaving the newcomer confused about what technique is most appropriate. Dr. Herbert Benson of Harvard Medical School reports that virtually every culture has developed means for inducing what he calls the relaxation response. However, many yogis and others with extensive meditation experience see it as a process which vastly eclipses relaxation. The basic techniques of meditation have been practiced for thousands of years. A Christian treatise from the fourteenth century recommends the repetition of a single syllable word such as "God" or "love." Francisco De Osuna's tenth century work, *Third Spiritual Alphabet*, describes the practices of mystics who sought to achieve union with God through the silent repetition with each breath of "Lord Jesus have mercy on me."[1] The Yoga sutras of Patanjali, which are said to date back to the sixth century B.C., describe the process of consciously uniting with one's true Self through the preliminary practices of sense withdrawal, restraint of breath, and concentration leading to *samadhi*, a state in which the mind is totally still.[2] Similar instructions can be found in other traditions—including Hinduism, Buddhism, Judaism, Taoism, and Shintoism.

Secular variations of these methods can be seen today in such techniques as relaxation training, autogenic training, or biofeedback. Researchers report a wide range of benefits which have been gained from the practice of the relaxation response: significant lowering of blood pressure in hypertensive patients; reduction of the frequency and intensity of pain; and help with any condition set off by the fight or flight response, which is the body's reaction when alarmed or stressed.[3]

Meditation is essential for anyone engaged in the process of self-generated healing. There are many specific benefits. Our actions and habits can obstruct our efforts to promote the healing process. People who meditate find habits less difficult to change. Furthermore, meditation can help you induce your own healing. Even with the sophisticated diagnostic and treatment techniques of modern medicine, Benson states that doctors today are successful in treating only 25% of the illnesses which patients bring to their offices. Many of the other 75% are caused by the effects of complex mind-body interactions. Meditation can help reduce the stress and anxiety of daily life, which can retard the healing process after medical interventions such as drugs or surgery.[4] Kenny, a PWA, said at a recent seminar:

> There are times when I'm very tired and I feel, "No, I don't want to make dinner. I'd rather just stay in bed." I find that with meditation, if you just close your eyes for five minutes and put yourself back *here* for five minutes, all of a sudden you'll find the energy to make dinner. Otherwise, it would have been a chore. Your energy goes down and down. You might get dinner made, but not eaten. After five minutes of meditation, I remember that this is not a chore, it's something that I enjoy doing. You

don't have to meditate for hours and hours. Five minutes should do it. Just putting yourself back in the center of yourself.

The most important reason for meditating goes beyond practical considerations. AIDS requires you to face the greatest challenges in life: disease, social isolation, the loss of loved ones, death. Rather than hiding from these challenges or going through them kicking and screaming, why not face them with the comfort of a calm, clear mind? This becomes possible only if you take the time to regularly experience the peacefulness which is within you. This recharge through silence will come to be experienced as a basic need, in some ways like our need for food, shelter and love. There is a sign outside a Las Vegas gambling casino which says "You have to be present to win." That statement embodies the reason for meditation. Most people's minds are so busy and unfocused that they are not present. They do not experience what is happening in the present moment, and as a result, they do not win—that is, reach their goals, restore health, establish good relationships, etc.

Laying a Foundation for Meditation

Meditation is a twenty-four hour-a-day process; not a discrete twenty minute process separate from the rest of your life. Mindfulness or one-pointed awareness are terms which refer to the state of consciousness in which the mind is focused, relaxed, and present. An ongoing mindfulness is required to make meditation a continuous experience.

Established meditation guidelines uniformly stress the importance of an ethical foundation as a basis for meditation practice. As Kornfield states, "If we are engaged in actions that cause pain and conflict to ourselves and others, it is impossible for the mind to become settled, collected, and focused in meditation; it is impossible for the heart to open."[5]

The first of these ethical guidelines is non-violence in

thoughts, words, and deeds. Angry thoughts have an obvious unsettling effect on the mind; repressing anger also takes its toll on a person. The goal is to be aware of the anger without being tossed about by it. Learning to understand and appropriately express anger when necessary is a process which takes most individuals many years. Another guideline is truthfulness—dishonesty fragments our awareness because we are pulled in different directions simultaneously. Talking is a way in which much energy can be wasted, either by saying what is untrue or what is not particularly important. It is beneficial to have periods of silence as well as to bring more awareness to what we say. Stealing or hoarding more than we need is inconsistent with establishing a deeper spiritual life. Intoxicants cause a cloudiness in the mind which makes meditation very difficult. Similarly, other excesses—for example, with food or with sexual behavior—can deplete the energy which we bring to our inner life. These guidelines are not presented from a judgmental vantage point; rather they describe the ways of living which are consistent with the deepening of an inner awareness. There are many people who do not meditate formally but are at peace with themselves because they follow these guidelines, without intending them as meant for spiritual development. Conversely, people who meditate but continue to lead unethical lives remain troubled.

Another practice which enables meditation to be a twenty-four hour-a-day process is making a conscious effort to keep your awareness focused in the present moment. It is so easy to approach AIDS with thoughts of, "What's *going to* happen? Will my T cells go down? Will my KS spread? Will I have to go back in the hospital? Will I survive the year?" Whenever you notice yourself doing this, try to shift your awareness to "What *is* happening? I'm listening to music. I'm writing. I'm walking. I'm eating a muffin." This deceptively simple practice is the basis of meditation in action.

The Process of Meditation

I recommend that you approach periods of meditation with a framework of four basic stages. This is not a new technique, just a way of understanding what you are doing when you sit down to meditate. The stages are: quieting the noise, stating your purpose, silence and completion. Each of the four stages is necessary. When I have found that a meditation was not effective, usually it is because the purpose of one of these four stages was not accomplished. For example, I did not quiet my mind at first and was therefore unable to make any real focussing possible. Or, I did not stop to remind myself of why I was sitting there. Or, I did not sit still in silence, but moved about and made limited effort to stay with the object of concentration. Or, finally, I jumped up after meditating without any closing thoughts or prayers. Each step will be discussed separately and can be adapted in your own way. What is recommended is that the basic purpose of each step be incorporated in your meditation practice.

Step One: Quieting the Noise

Begin the period of meditation by calming down. Most people in industrialized countries have acclimated themselves to life with a significant amount of tension in the body. The practice of yoga goes from the gross (the actions of daily life, the body) to the subtle (the nature of thought). In order to do this delicate work with the mind, it is necessary to have ease in the body. Do a few gentle stretches, slowly and coordinated with the breathing. Listening to music can calm the mind. Deep muscle relaxation dramatically reduces tension. The breath is a bridge between the body and mind. A good way to quiet thoughts is by regulating the breath with several deep inhalations and gradual exhalations.

Begin your meditation by mentally scanning the body for any tension. You can relieve the tension by gently stretching the muscles in that area or by simply bringing your awareness to it. If the tension or restlessness does not subside, lie down and do a deep relaxation. You can do this on your own or by following the recorded instructions on a cassette. Then watch your breath—breathing through your nose deeply to the abdomen. Count ten to fifteen breaths. Let the stillness become more and more pervasive.

Step Two: Statement of Purpose (to Let Go)

The purpose of this second step is to take the time to reflect on why you are meditating and how you can make best use of the time. As Swami Satchidananda says, "If you want God to come in, make room." We are making room to see things differently. It is easy for spiritual practice to become part of a routine—carried out regularly but without much feeling. Here, we state our willingness to release our automatic thought process. It is for this reason of making room that people light candles, invoke the presence of a spiritual guide, or put flowers on a table. It is also a good idea to state your intention to be closed to the outside world during the period of meditation. For example, if you repeat a mantra, say to it, "For these twenty minutes, it's just me and you." If you like a particular prayer from your own religious tradition, say the prayer at this time—slowly, carefully, aware of the meaning of each word.

Some people are comfortable with religious language; others are not. A friend who worked on a hospital psychiatric unit told me of her conversation with a patient. The patient kept saying that she would be fine "if only she could surrender to Jesus." My friend said that for her the idea of surrendering to Jesus was not meaningful, "but I know what it means to genuinely let go and open myself to a new way of seeing things. It was through that experience that I was able to identify with the patient." The purpose of this second step is to "make room" for a peaceful presence inside yourself.

Step Three: Silence

Henri Nouwen writes that "The Russian mystics describe prayer as descending with the mind into the heart and standing there in the presence of God."[6] Steps One and Two were the "descent" into the heart; Step Three represents the "standing there."

Unfortunately, the mind is not easily silenced. Ram Dass offers the following description:

> Thought after thought with the rapidity of a trip hammer. Thoughts about what you hear, what you

> taste, what you smell, what you see, what you feel, what you remember, what you plan. On and on they go, a raging, roaring river of thoughts pouring through you: "think of me, think of me, think of me, me, me, me, me first, think of me." And so it goes all day, till you go to sleep.[7]

It usually takes a while before the mind even begins to stand still. Because most people find a meditation on thoughtlessness too abstract, I recommend that you choose one object or thought on which to focus your mind. The two suggestions in choosing an object of meditation are that it be uplifting and something which the mind likes. The focus can be on a mantra; or on the breath; or on a picture or mind of a great soul; or on an image from a dream; or, according to Patanjali, anything that is elevating. You should not keep changing your object of concentration. As Swami Satchidananda says, "There's no point in digging shallow wells in a hundred places. Decide on one place and dig deep." You could use a mantra, which is a sound formula for meditation—examples are "Hari Om" or "Om Shanti" or the English words "Be Still." Benson reports that eighty percent of the patients he works with choose a prayer to repeat during meditation. He contends that the "support of personal beliefs make the technique easier to practice."[8] Christians may repeat "Hail Mary. Full of grace." or "The Lord is my shepherd." Jews may choose either the Hebrew word for "peace," *shalom*, or "one," *echod*. The repetition can be spoken, whispered, or repeated mentally, which is the most subtle. It is most beneficial to say the words with both concentration and feeling. When the mind wanders, notice that and return to the object of concentration. The process consists of focusing again and again. Once stillness is established, let go of the object of concentration and sit in the silence. During this period of silence, sit absolutely still. Try not to move your body at all. If you can sit upright, cross-legged without a chair, then do so. If you need a chair, use a chair. If you are unable to sit up, it is okay to meditate in a lying down position. However, you run the risk of falling asleep.

Set aside a specific period of time—perhaps ten minutes twice a day, at first. Then gradually increase the length of time. The saying in theatre, "Always leave them wanting more," applies with meditation. It is good to stop meditating before the mind gets so restless that your memory of meditating is one of impatience and frustration. People rarely continue doing what they do not enjoy. If approached with gentleness and perseverance, meditation will bring an indescribable joy.

Step Four: Completion

Don't jump up when the period of silence is over. Thoughts are powerful when the mind is quiet. This is an opportune time for sending thoughts for the well-being of others and for your own health and spiritual realization. It is also a good time to review the day—whether it is beginning or just past. Stay seated until you feel that you have given a genuine blessing to yourself and others.

❖

Those who themselves have journeyed on the path of meditation and guided others on their way have offered helpful observations about obstacles or hindrances which have most frequently been encountered. The Buddha taught that "Those who conquer their own minds are greater than those who conquer a thousand men a thousand times in battle." Buddhist meditation instructions warn of five major hindrances: desire, aversion, sloth and torpor, restlessness, doubt. Sometimes these hindrances surface one at a time, but they can pounce in a "multi-hindrance attack." Desires keep the mind moving—operating with the belief that the moment will be satisfying only when a given event occurs. The purpose is not to live without goals or pleasures—but to keep a balance through all of life's experiences. The experience of aversion—which can take the form of anger, dislike, or resentment—has an immediate unsettling effect on the mind. Sloth and torpor bring a clouded state of mind which works against meditation. Restlessness can be a constant demon for a meditator. Doubts can ultimately cause a practitioner to stop meditating altogether.[9]

Be aware of these obstacles in your own practice. It is better to say "Oh, there's desire. I'm thinking about a slice of pizza" than to think of the pizza, stop meditating and head for the nearest pizza parlor. Other examples: "There is anger. Okay, now I'll try to let the wave of anger pass through my mind and body and then return to the meditation." Or, "I've started having doubts about meditation, and I'm thinking that it's a waste of time." If you have made an agreement with yourself to meditate each day, keep your agreement. If you feel too tired or too restless to meditate, meditate anyway. If you're falling asleep, you can try standing up. A few years ago, I made a promise with myself to meditate one hour a day. I was exhausted at the end of the day and the hour meditation seemed like forever. I was fighting off sleep continually, but remained seated throughout the hour, without giving in to the temptation of stopping and going to bed. That night I had a beautiful dream in which my spiritual teacher came to me and gave me a big hug.

Obstacles to meditation are so insidious. Ego is being challenged, and it won't give up without a fight. Ram Dass says:

> The ego has convinced us that we need it, not only that we need it, but that we are it. I am my body. I am my personality. I am my neuroses. I am angry. I am depressed. I am a good man. I'm sincere. I seek truth. I'm a lazy slob. Definition after definition... But as long as the ego calls the shots, we can never become other than what it says. Like a dictator, it offers us paternalistic security at the expense of our freedom.... But meditation does work. It gives you moments of sunlight, of clarity and detachment. Sooner or later, you must either stop meditation, do it in a dishonest way, or confront your resistance to change.[10]

It is good to discuss your experiences in meditation with a teacher or experienced meditator. Also, keeping a journal in which experiences during meditation are recorded is also useful. Ramana Maharshi stated that "If one wants to abide in a thought-free state, a struggle is inevitable."[11] Thomas Merton echoed that sentiment. "True love and prayer are learned in the hour when love becomes impossible and the heart has turned to stone."[12] These dry periods have been part of everyone's experience. Encouragement can be found in knowing that they often precede breakthroughs.

Eight

Imagery and Healing

❖

We live in a world which uses lasers to remove cataracts and dissolves kidney stones with ultrasonic rays. With such sophisticated medical technology available, the idea that your health can be improved by focusing on specific mental images might sound preposterous. Peter Pan used imagery techniques when he told Wendy and Michael to "think lovely thoughts" in order to fly. Even that might sound more plausible than using your own mental images to cure diseases that you can barely pronounce—such as pneumocystis carinii, cytomegalovirus, or even candida albicans. Nonetheless, the many personal experiences shared during the visualization workshops I have led over the past years have convinced me of the very important role imagery plays in your emotional, physical and spiritual well-being.

Images are inner representations of a memory or fantasy. They occur in all sensory modalities—sight, sound, touch, etc. They often flash across the screen of your consciousness in such rapid succession that you rarely have any control or awareness of the process. In order to use imagery techniques effectively, the activity of your imagination must come within your conscious awareness. Imagery techniques are usually done with a specific goal in mind—for example, deepening our understanding of a troublesome relationship; gaining insight into a personal problem; or directing healing energy toward an illness. Imagery techniques can be used either actively (consciously generating specific images) or passively (allowing images into consciousness which have previously been subconscious). Most people associate imagery techniques exclusively with the visual. However, not all imagery practices are visualizations. For example, you may enter into a state of deep relaxation and spontaneously hear words or music which have a profound impact.

We all use imagery techniques both consciously and unconsciously. An obvious example is salivating when we think of tasty food. Any fearful thought is an aversive response to an anticipated image. If you do not look forward to work on Monday, you have images in your mind which make work seem unappealing. Similarly, looking forward to a date on Saturday is a positive reaction to the images of anticipated events. Imagery techniques can be as simple as thinking of a loved one, recalling a taste of a delicious apple, mentally recreating the sounds of beautiful music, or recollecting special moments during a recent vacation. Behavior therapists use imagery to treat phobias, the advertising industry to sell merchandise. We all live with images about the people and events in our life. It is these images which can limit our possibilities for fulfillment, not the people or events themselves.

How is it possible to consciously use mental images to promote physical healing? You may have seen people on TV talking about visualization techniques: space ships destroying a brain tumor or ferocious dogs eating cancer cells. But imagery techniques are far more than the latest fad from Southern California. In her book, *Imagery in Healing*, Jeanne Achterberg states that imagery is the oldest healing technique known to man. She offers a thorough review of the seminal role imagery techniques have played in the healing process in diverse cultures from around the globe—from Native American, Tibetan, Catholic Mystics to a friendly country doctor. Achtenberg quotes Thomas Largewhiskers, a 100-year-old Navajo Indian medicine man: "I don't know what you learned from books, but the most important thing I learned from my grandfather is there's a part of my mind we don't really know about and that is that part that is most important in whether we become sick or remain well."[1] Einstein said that his creative brainstorms did not come from his "mind," but from another place entirely:

> The words or the language, as they are written and spoken, do not seem to play any role in my mechanism of thought.... The...entities which seem to serve as elements in thought are...more or less clear images which can be 'voluntarily' reproduced and combined.[2]

The different books about imagery which are on the market today offer varied but not necessarily inconsistent explanations of how the imagery process works. Psychologist Arnold Lazarus, in *In the Mind's Eye*, states that mentally rehearsing an action prepares one to do it in real life. For example, you are flooded with anxiety at the thought of walking across a room and asking someone to dance. A mental rehearsal would involve learning deep relaxation and then, once relaxed, picturing yourself going up to the person, asking him or her to dance, and preparing your responses to either being accepted or rejected.[3] Sports psychologist Daniel Landers concluded, after an extensive review of research on the effectiveness of visualization in athletic competition, that mental rehearsals before athletic events do in fact improve performance.[4]

Other books offer a metaphysical explanation of the imagery process. They see the universe, which is fundamentally made of energy and thoughts, as a subtle but powerful force molding a person's life. Thoughts are seen as having the power to become manifest in real life. This idea is not unique to contemporary metaphysical thinkers. It is expressed in the Buddhist saying, "You are what you think, having become what you thought," and the Yoga teaching, "As you think, so you become." The events of our life are seen as being guided by a mental law of attraction—meaning that we attract people and events into our world according to the dominant characteristics of our psychological structure. People are seen as reaping what they sow with their thoughts. That is, angry thoughts produce angry events and thoughts of charity produce charitable consequences, etc.

This position can be taken to extremes and is an aspect of New Age philosophy which is quite controversial. Many PWAs, understanding these ideas to suggest that they wanted AIDS, vigorously reject this—saying that they want to live and do not believe they brought this tragic event into their life. They acknowledge moments of insecurity, but do not see themselves as more self-critical than others who are not in high-risk groups and, therefore, are not facing an early death. It is shallow-minded to say that gay people en masse have invoked this epidemic upon themselves because of a lack of self-love or internalized homophobia. Shirley MacLaine said that on her fiftieth birthday she mentally projected the success of *Terms of Endearment*, her Oscar, a best-selling book, and a Broadway show. These events all came to pass, according to her, because she succeeded at clearing her mind of all doubt and fear and then visualized success. Was she saying that the Oscar goes to whomever visualizes the best? Certainly talent and promotion play a part. Is the presidential election won by the candidate who does imagery techniques with most perseverance and focus? It would be beneficial for a presidential candidate to mentally rehearse all the possible events which could occur, for example, in a debate, and to make himself genuinely comfortable with the images of being President; the resulting confidence would most likely favorably impress the voters. But the final outcome of an election is determined by a great many factors.

I believe that thoughts do matter in ways that most people do not recognize. If you meditate regularly or have studied your dreams, you have probably discovered that your thoughts are potentially very powerful and are often interconnected with the thoughts of others. Nevertheless, your life span is governed by events which are beyond your understanding. What is necessary is to clean up your own mind, and make it a clear vehicle for loving, healing thoughts. While it may seem far-fetched that people cause their tumors, their childrens' diseases, or epidemics in their communities, do not neglect the importance of your own thoughts in determining your future.

Rossman, a physician, offers a more physiological explanation of why imagery works. He sees imagery as a way of making use of the brain's right hemisphere, which uses images and processes information simultaneously rather than sequentially.[5] The right brain has the ability to grasp the larger context of events and may be what Largewhiskers is referring to when he speaks of "part of our brain that we don't really know about."

Imagery for many people has a spiritual dimension. They experience images of Christ, Buddha, spiritual teachers, or departed loved ones. For these people, imagery is approached as a spiritual practice. Whether imagery is understood as a healing process due to right hemisphere involvement, a spiritual visitation, a metaphysical phenomena, or a behavioral rehearsal, the important thing is to do it.

❖

The following guidelines are offered to help you have the most beneficial experience with imagery exercises.

You must be relaxed

Some people think being relaxed means having a few drinks by a pool. What is meant here is a deep muscle relaxation in which tension in the body markedly declines, the thought process slows down, yet awareness remains alert. Some relaxation tapes state that you gain all the benefits of relaxation subliminally even if you fall asleep during the relaxation process. You will sleep well, but imagery is a meditative process which requires awareness. Relaxation enables you to be more aware of your thought patterns and provides the quality of mind which is necessary for effective imagery. I do relaxation exercises with an audio-cassette tape.

Once the techniques are memorized, you can proceed without the tape. The process of relaxation involves first tensing and relaxing all the major muscles, then bringing the awareness to the breath and finally focusing on an experience of peacefulness which enables you to observe rather than identify with thoughts. It is at this point that the ground is laid for either planting or unearthing clear and potent images.

Keep your awareness centered in the present moment

As Louise Hay says, "The point of power is always in the present moment."[6] The spiritual journey consists of bringing a gentle non-judgmental awareness to the specific challenges of each moment. Rarely does one make steady, uphill progress. When your mind jumps toward past or future events, you limit your healing capacity.

Repetition

Imagery exercises need to be done again and again. Some people speak of absorption in the imagery process, meaning absorbing certain images more and more deeply into their consciousness. We grew up hearing biblical stories of healing happening in an instant. But Father Francis MacNutt writes in his book, *The Power to Heal*, that in his experience healing is a far more gradual process.[7] The founders of Unity, Reverend and Mrs. Filmore, prayed several times a day during a two year process before their medical conditions were cured. I remember hearing of a PWA who stopped all health-promoting activities after having a meditation experience which convinced him that his body had been healed. Unfortunately, he died several months later. The process of visualization requires perseverance and continual fine-tuning.

Support from others

A fourth guideline is that you seek support in the process by finding a partner, joining a support group, or working with a guide or counselor with experience in the use of imagery and healing. People realize that they need instruction to help them learn to lift weights or plant a garden, but somehow feel that reading a spiritual book is sufficient training for meditative work. The human mind is very tricky, and rarely does one make progress when working alone. People have friends for going out on the town and partying but sometimes approach their spiritual life in solitude. That may work for a determined individual with much inner direction, but you run the risk when going it alone of giving up when frustrated or not making the progress that perhaps could be made.

Keep a Journal

You will learn a great deal by writing about your experiences with the visualization process. A daily journal is strongly recommended. Often you lose perspective. You may find visualization to be boring and ineffective on Thursday and Friday, forgetting that a very powerful experience occurred several days earlier. By having your experiences on paper, you become aware of overall trends. The next step on the journey becomes evident when you can read about your previous experiences.

Be Original and Think Big

Imagery practices are at their best when they are unique to a given individual. I have heard of a plumber who effectively visualized an improved heart by picturing pipes being cleared out. A heavy equipment operator visualized a house-lifting jack separating his vertebrae. A nun pictured St. Teresa of Licieux dropping flower petals, and a housewife saw a potent cleaning solution scraping away her endometriosis. A woman struggling with inertia pictured galloping horses in order to get herself going.

Often imagery techniques involve thoughts of healing rather magically. For example, white light is eliminating a tumor, or the spirit of Jesus is blessing you. People may think this type of occurrence is possible in the lives of certain special people, but that it is not a viable possibility in their own lives. The *thought* that it is not going to occur can often be a barrier to the healing process. Fix your mind on an image of wholeness until it becomes a reality. Those who practice Christian healing teach that with anything you ask and pray for, believe that you have it already and it will be yours.[8] Sometimes people in seminars are embarrassed when they tell stories of their visualization experiences, seeming apologetic about the images they had. It is essential that you realize that there is a benevolent presence or awareness which is available to you and can offer healing, comfort and wisdom.

❖

I have read and have personally attempted hundreds of imagery exercises. The annotated bibliography includes books which offer specific imagery techniques for a wide range of purposes (for example, healing, spiritual understanding, achieving a goal, making money, winning back an ex-lover, etc.).

Two imagery techniques will be presented in detail. You are encouraged to develop both of these techniques. The first involves finding an image of a specific illness and then another image of how the healing of that illness is represented. Rossman reports contradictory findings concerning whether knowledge of physiology is necessary for effective visualization.[9] In the case of AIDS, learning the intricacies of the human immune system could take years of graduate study. However, it is useful to understand, for example, that the T4 cells initiate immune response. The T4 cells have been called the quarterback of the immune team or the conductor of the immune symphony. During these imagery exercises we will picture the HIV-virus as weak and confused and the T4 cells as strong, independent and prolific. These imagery exercises can be done quickly throughout the day and also during specific extended periods. The second technique involves imagery techniques in which you establish a relationship with an inner guide—the teacher inside you. Both techniques are extremely valuable in aiding the self-healing process. You can make your own recording of these imagery excercises or purchase the cassette which is available with this book.

Imagery Process on Illness and Health

We will very gently and patiently relax the entire body. Lie down on your back with your palms up, feet about eighteen inches apart, hands at your side. If your chin is jutting toward the ceiling, gently tuck it in toward your chest. Inhale deeply. As you exhale, release tension. You will be tensing and relaxing different parts of the body. As you inhale, you tighten the muscles, then hold the inhalation as the muscles are tightened more and more. Finally, as you exhale, let the air gush out through the mouth, and relax the part of the body which you had tightened.

Let us begin with the right leg. Bring your awareness to the right leg. Tense it, inhale. Raise the leg a few inches off the floor. Tighten the muscles, tighter, tighter. Exhale. Release.... Bring your awareness to the left leg. Inhale. Tense the leg. Raise the leg up, tighter, tighter. Exhale. Release.... Inhale. Stretch the fingers of the right hand. Raise the arm up a few inches off the floor. Make a fist. Tighten the arm, tighter, tighter. Exhale. Relax the arm.... See that the limbs fall down to the ground, totally relaxed. Inhale. Stretch the fingers of the left hand. Raise the arm up. Make a fist. Tighten the arm, tighter, tighter. Release.... Now inhale. Tense the buttocks, tighter, tighter. Release.... Bring your awareness to the abdomen. Inhale. Puff up your stomach. Expand it, more and more. Raise the abdomen. Exhale and release.... Inhale. Expand the chest. Fill the chest as much as possible, more, more, and exhale.... Now let your head fall from side to side as you relax the muscles of the neck.... Now inhale. Tense all the facial muscles. Tighten the face up into a prune face, tighter, tighter, and release.... Now mentally scan your body, seeing that all the tension is released. By using the power of your awareness, allow a wave of peacefulness to sweep across your entire body. Relax your toes, your feet, calves, knees, thighs and buttocks. (Pause) Relax your fingertips, hands, wrists, forearms, elbows and upper arms. (Pause) Now release at the base of the spine, hips and pelvis, lower back, abdominal area, rib cage, across the shoulder blades and the muscles between the shoulder blades, the shoulders, across the collar bone to the neck and the head. (Pause) See that your face is relaxed, being sure to relax the jaw, the eyes, the cheeks, the mouth. Bring a wave of peacefulness to your brain. Scan the body, making sure that it's completely relaxed.... Now observe the breath. Don't control the breath. Just watch it. The breath should be shallow. Be aware of the inner stillness. (Pause 2-3 minutes) Now bring your awareness to your immune system. The AIDS virus is a *tiny* piece of information that can not grow or multiply unless it finds a home. The home it seeks is on the helper T cells. These T cells are born in the bone marrow. So bring a loving, healing energy to your bones. Picture different sets of cells bursting forth from the bone marrow into the blood stream. The helper cells mature and take shape in the thymus gland, located in the center of the chest. Picture many helper T cells emerging from the thymus gland. They are strong, with an *impenetrable* surface, disguised so they can not be recognized by the HIV-virus. See the HIV-virus becoming weaker and more and more isolated. The helper T cells are *truly helpers*. They are the quarterback, or the conductor of the symphony of your immune system... Also bring life and energy to your killer T cells, which attack any enemy with perfect aim. And bring your energy and loving awareness to the suppressor T cells, which quiet down the work of the immune system when the job is done. Bring energy and healing to the B cells, which manufacture antibodies that stick to invaders so it is easier for other cells to attack them. And direct a healing energy from your conscious mind to the scavenger cells, which sweep the body clean, working slowly and thoroughly, eliminating every trace of danger, including fungus and bacteria. Picture the HIV-virus becoming weaker and weaker, more and more isolated, and finally eliminated from your system—leaving strong and intact T4 cells and the entire immune system in good shape. Each day you are creating more and more T4 cells.... (Pause 1-2 minutes) Relax with the knowledge that your immune system is repairing itself....

Now turn your awareness toward any specific illness—however you understand it right now, whatever symptoms there are. Look at it with compassion. What images come to your mind as you consider your illness? Picture it realistically or symbolically. Stay with those images, feel them. Notice the tendency of your mind to judge, to comment. Let the images become clearer and clearer. Approach this process with a peaceful, accepting mind. (Long pause)

Now consider your healing. What image of healing comes to your mind? Stay with that image, look at it in every dimension, from different angles. Stay with the image and appreciate it. Let it fill your consciousness. Think of all that healing entails, how the entire person is involved. (Long pause)

Now look at the images of healing and of the illness together. Which is more powerful? Is it possible for the image of healing to become stronger than the image of the illness? What does that entail? Picture your immune system eliminating the illness. What does it require of you? Stay with the images. Thank them. Reflect on your willingness to learn from these images. Rest peacefully. (Long pause)

We will be ending this meditation soon, but before we stop, let's pause and once again bring health to your entire body. See that your skin is healthy and clear.... Be aware of your entire gastrointestinal tract. Picture that the inside of your mouth is clean and healthy and without any blemishes. See that your esophagus is also healthy. Feel that your stomach is relaxed, that the intestines absorb everything in the food which is needed for health and comfortably eliminate what is not needed.... Be aware of your lungs. Bring health to your lungs. Breathe freely, with the knowledge that your respiratory system is strong and healthy.... Picture that your entire nervous system, from the brain all the way through every nerve ending, is functioning perfectly. See that your nerves in your arms and legs, hands and feet, are all functioning perfectly....Bring health to your entire body.

Keep your awareness within. The mind and body are quiet. Ask for blessings for improved health. Bathe in the healing force of these blessings. Watch your breath for several inhalations and exhalations and then gently open your eyes.[10]

It is very important to take time to reflect on your imagery experience, perhaps by writing in a journal. This process is most beneficial when done frequently and when followed with a period of reflection. Did you have clear images? What do you think these images are telling you? Could you draw these images? Try not to judge or evaluate your experience or compare it with those of others. Often people have simple experiences containing wisdom that they fail to recognize. Your capacity for imagery increases according to your practice and motivation. Rather than thinking about how other people's imagery might be better, try to be appreciative of the images that came to you and reflect on what these images are telling you. Most importantly, reflect on how you can make the image of healing a reality.

Inner Guide

There is much wisdom inside you. Swami Satchidananda says, "The greatest doctor is inside us. It is God or nature's energy." When facing illness, people can become panicked and, as they seek medical care, not listen to their own inner voice. A major concern for shamans was to understand what loss of personal power had occurred which permitted the intrusion of a particular disease in the first place. Some people think of their inner guide as a spiritual guide, others as a wise elder or the spirit of God. The mind needs an image to personify or represent its highest aspiration. It is very beneficial to have images in your consciousness with which you can discuss your innermost concerns. In order to remain focused, you need an image—for example, a spiritual teacher, or a relative who has died, or a flower, or a candle flame. Buddha taught that people should look within themselves for wisdom rather than worship icons. Ironically, more shrines have been built for Buddha than any other master. I have visited temples which are said to contain a part of his tooth or collarbone. People need sacred images.

The purpose of the following process is to help you consciously access your own inner advisor. Actual images may change over time and according to your particular needs. A spiritual guide may provide counsel on a meditation journey, while a beloved uncle may provide advice about a troubled marriage.

Inner Guide Imagery Process

We begin by gently stretching and relaxing the body. Lie down on your back on a fairly firm surface, perhaps on a towel on a carpeted floor. Inhale and exhale slowly, taking approximately ten breaths with as much awareness as possible.

Now inhale and stretch your arms up overhead. Reach the fingers as far from you as you can, while you point your toes. Stretch. Exhale and release, leaving the arms overhead. We will repeat. Stretching your fingertips and the tips of your toes, reaching more and more, exhale and release. Return your hands to your side. Now inhale and bend your knees, bringing your thighs up to your chest. Wrap your arms around your legs and bring your forehead up to meet your knees. Hold for 15-20 seconds and then lie down and relax. Now let the body relax further. You will tense and relax the entire body at once, lifting the body up into a slightly V-position as you hold the breath. Then you will release the body and breath simultaneously. So inhale, tense the arms, legs, buttocks. Lift the legs and chest up off the floor. Tighten the arms, the face, the abdomen, the shoulders, the entire body, as you hold the breath. Now exhale, and release. We'll be repeating this quick relaxation. Inhale. Tense the arms and legs. Lift the body up into a V. Tight, tighter, tensing the entire body, including the face, the shoulders, the buttocks, exhale and release. Now let the body relax completely down onto the floor. You will use the power of your awareness to scan the body for any remaining tension. Relax your toes, your feet, calves, knees, thighs and buttocks. (Pause) Relax your fingertips, hands, wrists, forearms, elbows and upper arms. (Pause) Now release at the base of the spine, hips and pelvis, lower back, abdominal area, rib cage, across the shoulder blades and the muscles between the shoulder blades, the shoulders, across the collar bone to the neck and the head. (Pause) See that your face is relaxed. With the power of your awareness, scan the body, making sure that it's completely relaxed....

Now observe the breath. Try not to control the breath. The breath should be shallow. Be aware of the inner stillness. If the mind wanders, notice that and go back to watching the breath. Observe each inhalation and exhalation. Pause. Give in to the peacefulness—more and more and more.

Now picture yourself in a place of true beauty; a place you cherish, your home, a temple, a beautiful natural setting, perhaps on a beach or in the mountains. Appreciate the scenery. Notice the sights, sounds, smells. Be relaxed and fully aware of your surroundings. (Long pause)

Now ask for your inner guide to join you. Remain relaxed and notice whatever image spontaneously appears. Greet the guide in whatever way is appropriate—an embrace, prostration, handshake. Make the guide comfortable. Remember that this guide loves you and sincerely wants you to be healthy, wants a complete healing, and has the knowledge and wisdom to guide you in becoming healthier and in learning to face the challenges which the illness presents. You might mentally offer a seat or something to eat or drink. Again, anything that's appropriate.

Now, thank the guide for joining you and explain what is on your mind. Speak without any inner censors. Say what's in your heart. Don't try to impress the guide with your wisdom or your ability to hold things together. Just tell the truth. Discuss the concerns one at a time. Most importantly, be sure to tell the guide sincerely how you feel. (Pause 2 minutes) You might ask him or her what you need to do to be healthy. (Pause 1-2 minutes) What you need to do to be who you really are; to experience less fear, more hope, to be more peaceful. (Pause 2 minutes) No question is too large or too small. Don't rush through the conversation with the Inner Guide. Take all the time you need. Remember to listen patiently for a response. It may come immediately or it may come later. Be receptive. (Pause 1-2 minutes) Clarify any doubts that you

> might have. If you wish, bring up other issues. Again, discuss sincerely, clearly, from the heart. Listen to the response, not what you think the guide should say or would say, but what comes spontaneously, before you can actually program a response.
>
> When you are finished and are satisfied, thank the guide for joining you. Sincerely ask the guide for help in your efforts to be healthy and peaceful. Tell the guide that you need his or her continued love and friendship. Be sure to ask sincerely for its protection. Explain that you will be inviting him or her to return regularly in the future. Say goodbye in whatever way is appropriate. (Pause 1-2 minutes)
>
> Remain in the setting by yourself. Reflect on your experience with the guide. Consider what each of you said and felt. Consider what you need to do to strengthen your conscious connection with the guide.
>
> Slowly bring your awareness back to this room. Now be aware of your breathing and open your eyes.

Again, once the process is complete, don't jump up. It is important to reflect on what happened, what guide appeared before you. If the guide was not understanding or compassionate, try again and get someone who is more understanding. Reflect on your experience. Write down what happened.

The process of sharing openly what is in your heart is very healing. It is a great opportunity to learn and clarify your own feelings. Again, it can be useful to discuss with others who are experienced with this process, or an imagery partner, what your experience has been. Swami Satchidananda states "What is sacred should remain secret," meaning that these very personal experiences should only be shared with the people in your world who will be appreciative and respectful. He offers the following examples of healing imagery:

> In visualization, too, you are directing your prana

to the affected area. It's a form of meditation, because whatever you visualize, your entire mind is on that. It is even more powerful than physically doing or seeing something. You can do tremendous things with visualization.

You can practice visualization during deep relaxation, because at that time your body is more relaxed. Visualize something very natural: light, energy, energy from the sun, energy from the stars, energy from the ocean, ozone. The energy could be in the form of light, in the form of air, in the form of cool water. Feel that you are inhaling everything, that everything is coming into you, flooding into your system. Feel that the healing vibrations are coming from outside and going into and all over the body. And more particularly, wherever you feel the pain or the problem, feel that the healing energy goes to that point. Think of that area more.

For example, you could visualize a large ozonic wind on the surface of a big ocean. Feel that it's like a big cyclone, saying, "I'm coming into your system and bathing your whole body." Feel the ocean come in through your head and go down to the problem and out through your feet. It collects all the dirt and goes out, washing away the problems. You can even feel the cool breeze coming in with plenty of fresh energy and taking away all the toxins, going out as heat. It's all burnt out and it's going out—like fresh air coming in and going out as carbon dioxide.

You can visualize light. "All the light rays are coming into my body, burning all the unwanted cells, cleaning it up, charging everything with new energy."

Or you can imagine a divine being, like Jesus or Moses. Visualize them standing there in front of you, blessing you; and from their palms, energy is pouring into you. You feel the tingle all over. You can even feel that you are surrounded by all the great sages and saints. They are all around you, showering their energy upon you, blessing you.

You can create your own imagery. There's no fixed way. Choose whatever feels comfortable. You can heal your body just through your thinking. Every one of your thoughts has a certain power over your body. Isn't it true that the moment you think of a delicious candy your salivary glands act? That is how your thoughts affect your body. So think well, and you become well.

There are many other very useful imagery exercises. The most well-known is simply to consciously focus on a pleasant image. For example, while the dentist is drilling, you picture yourself on a beach. The purpose is to direct the awareness from an unpleasant situation to a more appealing picture. These images of beauty are often natural settings which you may have visited in the past and then recall frequently. If your home does not have any beautiful images, perhaps it is time to clean it up or add something new. It does not take a lot of money or an interior designer to have something of beauty in your home. It may be a flower or a chair or a bedside table. What is important is that you picture your home as a safe and beautiful place.

Another important imagery technique is what Lazarus calls the step-up technique, in which our fears are "stepped up" or exaggerated.[11] For example, I recall being very nervous about an upcoming case presentation. A friend of mine, after hearing me endlessly ruminate about the conference, said: "The worst that could happen is that you'll make a total fool of yourself and be fired." When she said this, I laughed. Being fired was not a likely occurrence, and making a total fool of myself would be less painful than continuing to live with fear. Another time I was sick while on a trip to India. Swami Satchidananda came into my hotel room, spoke with the doctor, and as he left said, "Well, we're not going to be able to take you out of Madras in a box. They don't make any big enough." Again, I laughed when he said this, realizing that I was far from being at death's door.

In 1966, Swami Satchidananda came to the United States and stayed briefly at the home of a New York City artist named Victor, who had to be at work every day, but was very concerned that Swamiji see New York City. In the morning when he would leave for work he told Swamiji about the Metropolitan Museum of Art, the Museum of Modern Art, the Museum of Natural History, etc. Each day found that the Swami had not gone out to any of these places. Finally, when he left for work one morning, he told Swamiji that he would come home that day and take him through Central Park and to a museum. Swamiji looked in his eyes, smiled, and said, "There are beautiful parks and museums inside me." When the artist heard this, his eyes filled with tears. He sensed the depth of experience from which Swamiji was speaking. Our meditations and imagery practices are designed to help bring us in touch with the beautiful parks and museums inside each of us. They can be found when sought with a patient, persistent effort.

Nine

The Power of Your Thoughts

❖

Have you ever established an exercise or diet regimen and then promptly violated the plan completely? Or been very enthusiastic about a job or relationship and then abruptly lost all interest? Or found yourself filled with self-doubt at times, yet realistically confident at others? Or sat down to meditate and then quickly got up having convinced yourself that meditation is a waste of time? Or angrily criticized a friend and, in so doing, damaged a relationship which you did not want to harm? These are common examples of inconsistency in our lives.

People are often eager to attempt the process of self-generated healing. Inspired by a book or a workshop, they attempt to put the ideas to work only to find themselves filled with skepticism and inertia a few days later. We often fail in efforts to convert intentions into consistent actions, discovering that our attitudes and feelings about life are constantly changing.

This chapter is about making friends with your own mind. The self-generated healing process requires a steady awareness of yourself throughout the day—not just during periods of meditation. This awareness will enable you to learn about the nature of your own resistance. Ondrea Levine describes this process as learning to "relate *to* rather than *from* our mind."

Most people do not understand that they are not their thoughts. Years ago I asked Swami Satchidananda for his advice concerning my going to graduate school in psychology. He said, "You will learn about the iron filings of the mind, but not about the magnet." The iron filings are the various thoughts in the mind. Graduate school would teach ways of organizing and sorting out these thoughts, but not about the magnet, which is the pure awareness or spirit. On another occasion, he was asked if he recommended that spiritual seekers watch movies. He responded that a spiritual seeker should always be watching the movie of his or her mind, "And if sometimes you want to watch a movie with a screen and projector, there is no harm in it." Our goal is to observe mental activity, rather than continually identify with its many variations. This point is further illustrated by Swamiji's response to a student who wrote him a letter saying that she was very bored and discouraged with life. She had wanted to be with him as much as possible and was working as his secretary, a job she had coveted for years. However, time passed and the job no longer interested her. After receiving the letter, he replied, "If you want excitement, go to Las Vegas. The only excitement for a spiritual seeker is to find something new in your mind to clean up."

If we are not our thoughts, then who are we? Ramana Maharishi, a 20th century Indian spiritual teacher, advised his students to continually ask the question, "Who am I?" as a means to realize their true identity. The following exercise may give you more understanding of the idea of the Self.

Identity Process

Write down on paper the following dimensions of your life:

- Begin with a life chronology on one piece of paper—date of birth, family background, education, work, any significant milestones—the events as they would appear in a brief biographical sketch.

- On a separate page write about the people in your life, those who have been important to you, those whom you have loved and been loved by.
- On another piece of paper write down the challenges that you have faced, the trials of life, (for example, family or personal problems, career setbacks, loss, illness)
- On another page, write down all your feelings about your body—what you have liked and not liked about it.
- On another page, write how you have seen yourself emotionally—happy, depressed, anxious, enthusiastic, etc.
- On another page, write down your experience with work, from jobs in high school through your career as an adult.

This exercise can be done with a partner. Rather than writing on paper, you will verbally explain each of the six categories to your partner, then reverse roles and hear these six dimensions of his or her life. Take about two minutes explaining each topic. When you are both finished, close your eyes for a brief meditation. Silently affirm that you are *not* your personal history, *not* your relationships, *not* your body image, *not* your struggles, *not* your emotions, *not* your career. You are the pure awareness that remains. Now do the same with your partner. Establish eye contact, and in silence remind yourself that he or she is not these six life dimensions, but is, in fact, that same pure consciousness. Spend some time silently sharing this awareness.

If you are doing this exercise alone, you can place the papers into a pile in front of you, and imagine the papers disappearing—just vanishing into the air. You can throw these papers away or, safety permitting, burn them. Who would remain? What is left?

The purpose of the identity process is two-fold: first, to get perspective on the different dimensions of your life; and secondly, to experience that there is a part of you that is independent from all these aspects. At a recent seminar, a man asked, "What about my individuality? my uniqueness? Are we all just pure awareness?" I answered by using one of Swami Satchidananda's analogies, the pieces in a game of chess. The rooks, bishops, knights, etc. all have a different form and specific rules to play by. But they are all made of the same wood and go back into the same box at the end of the game.

This same point was made in one of my most memorable interactions with Swami Satchidananda. During meditation initiation we were instructed to begin each meditation by invoking the presence and protection of our spiritual teacher. Part of my mind was puzzled by this. If Swami Satchidananda is in California or Hong Kong, engaged in whatever activities he is doing there, how can he protect me while I'm in New York? And what about the many other students all around the globe? I asked him about this. He spoke of the necessity of faith and told a story of a man who was refused instructions by a particular teacher. The student proceeded to build a clay statue of the teacher and received all the teachings from the statue. Swami Satchidananda then said, "Can I protect? It would be my ego that would say I cannot." I understood this to mean that if he identifies himself with his mind and body, he cannot protect. But if he identifies with the Self, then he—or anyone that experiences that Self—*is* protection.

When we believe that we are our own bodies, our histories, or our careers, we protect them desperately and stand to lose everything when their existence is threatened. Swami Sivananda, the teacher of Swami Satchidananda, said that, "any disease will take to its heels" when you affirm that "I am the bodiless, diseaseless all-pervading immortal soul or atman." This is a bold claim which is based on an experience that our minds find difficult to fathom.

We start by realizing that we are not our thoughts. The next stage is to gain a perspective on the different forms our mind takes. One world view with accompanying attitudes and beliefs may dominate our outlook on life only to be replaced by a totally different perception at another time. Psychosynthesis, a system of psychological and spiritual integration, explains this phenomenon with the term "subpersonalities." Each of us has many subpersonalities, each characterized by a particular dominant emotion or trait. A rebel may coexist with an obedient child. A committed lover might be at cross-purposes with a hedonist.

What is a subpersonality? The following exercise, derived from Ferrucci's *What We May Be*, should help you get to know your own subpersonalities. I recommend that you learn the steps of this exercise and do them frequently over a period of five or six weeks. Workshop participants find this exercise to be not only enlightening, but enjoyable. After years of being dominated by our subpersonalities, it is a freeing experience to hear them out, give them a name, and get perspective on them.

Recognizing Subpersonalities

(1) Consider one of your dominant emotions or outlooks toward life: fear, joy, mastery, incompetence, discouragement, mischievousness, etc. Think of a time when you have clearly been identified with this emotion or world view.

(2) Become increasingly aware of this part of you. Let an image appear which represents it. This image may be an aspect of yourself, a woman, man, child, literary figure, human or nonhuman, anything. Don't try to force an image, just let it appear.

(3) Let the image reveal itself to you. Get in touch with it. Learn the general emotion which emanates from it. Don't judge the image or the thoughts and ideas of it. Just get to know it as

it appears to you. Let it talk and express itself. Find out what it wants, its side of the story.

(4) Write down what you've learned. Make note of a name you might want to give this subpersonality, e.g. the Frightened Child, the Mule, "I Won't Play," the Temptress, the Rebel, the Escape Artist.

Once you've gotten to know this subpersonality, you can meet others by following the same steps.[1]

The reason for doing this exercise is to get perspective on the different parts of yourself without automatically identifying with them. As Ferrucci says, subpersonalities can be discovered by "taking stock of the various ways we look at life, by reviewing your behavior in various situations, and by considering your various styles of being you."[2] Once you get to know a subpersonality, you will be much more aware of times when you automatically identify with it. The idea is to experience the Self in the center and no longer reflexively assume the identities of these different personalities.

A group exercise illustrates this point. In this process, an individual explains five or six of his subpersonalities to the group. Each group member plays a different subpersonality, articulating its needs, its views and its perspectives, while the individual sits in the center of the room and mediates struggles between these various subpersonalities. This exercise would allow the Committed Lover to discuss why he sees benefit in fidelity, and the Hedonist could then voice his wishes and needs. The Lost Child could express its belief that no one will love him. The Narcissist would say why everyone is expected to admire him. The Stern Parent will warn against having too much fun.

What does this have to do with facing AIDS? An HIV-positive person I know has the subpersonality which he calls the Guru. This Guru feels a profound inner strength, knows the way to promote health, and has an inner faith which can sustain him through periods of illness. Co-existing with the

Guru is the Voice of Doom, who believes such things as, "It's too late, there's no hope" or "You've never succeeded at anything before, what makes you think you could succeed at something no one else has ever succeeded at?" The Voice of Doom has the ability to make the person forget about the Guru. And what makes this process even more insidious is that it happens without the conscious awareness of the person himself. This subpersonality exercise enables the individual to hear out the Voice of Doom and the Guru and get perspective on the different pulls these two subpersonalities have on him. Another seminar participant spoke of a subpersonality he calls the White Rabbit from *Alice in Wonderland*—always anticipating events but never experiencing them. By observing the White Rabbit, he became more able to focus his awareness on the present moment. By getting to know your subpersonalities, you will find that they lose their grip on your thoughts and actions.

Over the next few weeks, be aware of your own various outlooks on life. Who is the person who views life as a hopeless struggle? Who shrinks from challenges? Who enjoys beauty? Who connects with others? What is the name and face of the one who mistrusts others? Get to know these subpersonalities. Hear their side of the story without judgement. I have seen people become visibly uncomfortable when talking to one of their subpersonalities. "I hate that Awkward Teenager. I don't want to remember him." "The Angry Man is horrible. I don't like him. No one does." "That Lonely, Needy Woman would scare anyone off." A tremendous healing occurs when people can simply label and talk to their sub-personalities. So much energy is wasted in the futile effort to fight them off.

❖

What follows are several other techniques that I have found to be helpful in keeping the mind balanced and out of prolonged negative states. Don't focus on the "technique" to the degree that you forget the basic purpose—which is experiencing peace of mind. Two lessons from American history can help put this process in context. First is from the very recent past. Immediately after the 1988 Presidential Debates, "spinners" from the two candidates pounced on reporters to "spin" or interpret the debate in a way flattering to their candidate. The debate had occurred. Now the task was shaping how it would be understood by the viewer. Here the "spin" is to view the process of understanding the mind as enjoyable and possible, rather than overwhelming, frightening or impossible. The other lesson is a quotation from Abraham Lincoln: "Every man is as happy as he makes up his mind to be." Yet Lincoln experienced prolonged periods of depression. The moral: it's not easy.

The first technique is embodied just in the words *becoming friends with your own mind*. When you are upset about something, often your last thought is to be compassionate towards yourself for having this problem. If you have a relationship that has gone bad, or are filled with anger or fear, be kind with yourself about that very fact. Be kind with your mind and its fears. A very simple but enormously helpful technique is to adopt a non-judgmental, accepting attitude towards whatever you are feeling—whether it be a time of joy, sorrow, failure, success, being misunderstood, etc. A man went to a spiritual teacher and told him of his many insecurities. The master looked at him, smiled and said, "Doubting, doubting," and went on to say that doubting thoughts are just more thoughts to be observed. The problem with thoughts of self-doubt occurs only when you believe them and let them influence your emotions and behaviors. The goal is to see them, accept them, and continue the observation of whatever thoughts come up next.

A valuable means of learning to understand your mind is to get in touch with the different automatic thoughts that influence your moods and enjoyment in life. For example, some people repeatedly tell themselves that they are incompetent and can never do a job well. This thought can block effective job performance more than a lack of skills. Similar dysfunctional beliefs can interfere with relationships as well as healing. Research with cognitive therapy has shown that previously debilitating depressions are cured when people learn to identify and then respond to their automatic thoughts. We are often unconscious of these thoughts and therefore have no control over their effects. We don't hear ourselves saying, "I must be perfect." "He has to love me at every moment or we're finished." "If I stand up for myself, he will leave me."

The following questions, derived from psychologists Rakos and Schroeder, can be used to elicit underlying beliefs:

- Do you believe that you must be competent when engaged in important activities regardless of whether you have prior experience with the activity?

- Do you believe that all people who are very significant to you must always approve of you, love you, or else you feel that you are worthless? Is it okay if those people are disappointed or angry with you at times?

- Do you feel that you can have rights and self-worth without having earned them with specific achievements?

- When facing unresolved interpersonal conflicts, do you feel that inactivity is better in the long run than saying something that might "rock the boat"?[3]

Write down your responses to these questions. Make note of the ones which do not aid the self-generated healing process. These automatic thoughts can have the effect of limiting the healing process. One image which can visually express this idea is by recalling the fontanelle, which is the soft spot at the top of a baby's head. If you think of healing energy as coming into you through the crown of your head, you might also consider thoughts of depression and despair as being like a metal plate on top of your head, which prevent healing energy from entering.

After identifying your irrational automatic thoughts, the next step is thinking of a rational response to each one. A rational response is any thought that is reassuring for you and which is based on reason and not panic. In terms of facing AIDS, you may have thoughts that you must be perfect—eat the perfect food, see the right doctor, go to all the lectures. The pressure to be perfect interferes with healing. A rational response might be, "I am doing my best and will keep in touch with others who will keep me abreast of new ideas."

Often people think they should never make mistakes in handling difficult situations. Unfortunately, difficult situations are often new situations. What could be more difficult than having to face the prospect of death at an early age, possibly a painful death, while living in a society with much discrimination about the illness itself? It takes time before the challenge is met most effectively. Many people with AIDS are young and are used to being contributors to life. Their self-image is often based on an attractive and healthy body and an active, giving relationship to their society. When they become sick, this identity changes. They are often on the receiving end in relationships. Their physical and professional identity go through dramatic redefinitions. The rational response to thoughts of being useless might be a decision to learn from those who have contributed to others' lives while they had AIDS, or to see it as an opportunity to appreciate aspects of life which were not noticed before.

Another technique for working with the mind is what in the yoga sutras is called *pratipaksha bhavana*, meaning replacing a negative thought with its opposite. It is similar to what the cognitive therapists call thought-stopping. This might sound either impossible to do or totally repressive, but anyone I know who has given it a real try has been amazed at how well it works. The process is simple. If your mind is filled with an experience of thoughts which you consider negative, consciously tell yourself to stop those thoughts and consciously replace them with other, more positive thoughts, often opposite of what has just been troubling you. For example, a woman in a seminar recently told of driving to visit someone who in the past invariably had been rude and unpleasant. Shortly before arriving, she reminded herself of the thought-stopping exercise and decided to picture this person as friendly, outgoing, and generous in his words and actions. She suggested that the others in her car also try to see him in this positive light. They reluctantly agreed and were all startled to find that he was friendly—completely unlike how he had been on other occasions. He was approached with kindness and positive expectations and responded accordingly.

People will live up or down to your expectations. By choosing to fill your minds with certain thoughts and beliefs, you can unnecessarily make yourselves miserable. Begin by noticing the negative thoughts. Then firmly and decisively tell your mind to stop thinking that way. Finally, deliberately think thoughts that are completely different. There will be a few moments when you feel that you are swimming upstream, that you are reversing the natural momentum of your mind. In fact, you are. Once this shift in direction is established, a different perception will occur and you will feel much better.

Another important and useful way of controlling difficult and painful emotions is to make behavioral changes. If you are filled with anger about a situation, look at the clock and say, "It's 10:45 now, can I make it to 11:00 without being angry?" "Can I go for half an hour?" Tell your mind to let up on you for 15 minutes or half an hour. In her book, *Releasing*, Patricia Carrington has a suggestion for people who are holding onto a resentment which they feel that they just cannot release.[4] She suggests asking yourself if you can release one percent of the resentment. This one percent release is like going five minutes without letting your mind go into a groove of anger or resentment. It begins a process which makes a more thorough release possible. You might meet a friend and be afraid that the tension between the two of you will cause an argument to ensue. If you say to yourself, "I won't be in a fight. We will not argue. That just will not happen," you will be amazed at how that resolve will influence the interaction. In other words, by affirming that you have control of your behavior, not only do your behaviors change, the emotions and thoughts follow suit.

Yet another way of dealing with the mind is to learn from the examples of others. Reading biographies or watching movies about people's lives who embodied a certain characteristic helps build that quality. I remember attending a meeting of educators in South India. The speaker said that they would teach the life of Mahatma Gandhi—not as an Indian saint whose life was lofty and outside the reach of the students of India, but as a man who faced the same challenges as the children of India face today. Learn about the lives of people who you admire—whether they be your grandparent, a famous composer, a world leader, or the person living next door. By reflecting on the qualities of that person's life, you will absorb them to some degree. Modeling or imitation is a basic way that children learn. The single most important factor in determining if an adolescent will become a juvenile delinquent is whether his friends are juvenile delinquents. The saying, "Show me a man's friends and I'll know the man" makes the same point.

I hope that the preceding chapters on meditation and imagery made it clear that these are effective ways of changing your mental world. I have been amazed to see stubbornly held points of view evaporate through meditating, chanting, or doing a visualization process. A regular daily meditation practice is indispensable. The ideas contained in these chapters need to be implemented in order to make your mind your friend. Get to know your subpersonalities. Observe your automatic thoughts and develop rational responses to them. Only by applying these techniques will you gain the benefit of learning to enjoy your mind.

Ten

The Stages of Self-generated Healing

❖

How can we relate to disease in a way which is empowering and health-promoting? We have seen that healing does not occur at the physical level alone. Many people approach AIDS with only physical healing in mind. "If I beat AIDS I have won. If I don't I am defeated." This is limiting and ultimately is at cross-purposes with the healing process. If your attitude towards your body is "Get better and make it fast!" or you look at a KS lesion and say, "If it's not cleared up, I'm a failure," then you are approaching illness from a narrow perspective. The healing discussed in this chapter is at times symptom-directed, but it is not exclusively directed at symptoms. A symptom can be seen as a message to look at your overall approach to health.

Swami Satchidananda offers a framework which he calls the five steps of self-healing. In order to be effective, these practices need to be *ongoing* components of the self-generated healing process.

Stage One: Acceptance

Acceptance means facing a situation with honesty and responsibility. As Stephen Levine says, we are conditioned to put fear and resistance into our pain, illnesses, and failures. At the times when we are most in need of loving attention, we give ourselves just the opposite. The result can be that healing does not happen. Acceptance often entails turning around 180 degrees—directing your awareness towards a problem which you instinctively might have wanted to avoid.

I have seen a broad range of responses to an AIDS, ARC or HIV-positive diagnosis. These reactions range from depression to panic to a seemingly oblivious nonchalance. After initial HIV exposure, years can go by without any symptoms. Even after initial signs of HIV infection, more years can pass without any terribly painful or debilitating opportunistic infections. As a result, it is possible to forget that symptoms of a terminal disease could occur at any time. Acceptance of AIDS or ARC means an honest and compassionate awareness of this situation. It does not mean panic or terror. Nor does it mean burying your head in the sand.

Acceptance is an ongoing process. You practice it not simply in your relationship to AIDS, but by how you face the little setbacks that occur in daily life—missing a bus, being late to work, being concerned that a friend did not return a phone call, stubbing your toe. A balanced response to the the challenges of daily life prepares us to be accepting of greater challenges in the future.

Acceptance includes a dimension of repentance. Shamans' healing rituals have often begun with confession. The Catholic mass, which culminates in communion, a symbolic union with the divine, begins with calling to mind one's sins and asking for forgiveness. This is far more than a shame-inducing ritual. Our sins, or mistakes, are barriers which interfere with intimacy, with healing, and with spiritual insight. Acceptance means making peace with our past, or, in religious language, asking forgiveness for our sins. The Greek word, *metanoia*, is usually translated as 'conversion' or 'repentance.' It means not merely a change of manners but a change of heart—a change which is both personal and pervasive.

I understood what Swamiji means by repentance when

he spoke about his work with prisoners in Ceylon who had been in solitary confinement. He said that thirteen of the fourteen prisoners were released. Swamiji had helped these prisoners to see confinement to their cell as an opportunity for extended prayer and meditation. I asked him how they got out of jail. He replied, "Prayer. Some of them committed the crime, others did not. But they all repented, admitted their mistakes to God. Once they did that, amazing things happened. Witnesses would fail to appear in court, the prosecution would drop charges, and so on." Swamiji says repeatedly that your own conscience tells you what your mistakes are. Buddhists are taught to follow a middle path between strict asceticism and greed; similarly, Swamiji says that your mistakes are over-indulgences.

When the notion of repentance was presented at an AIDS seminar, the group became angry. One man said, "I have nothing to repent for. I'm not going to apologize for my life. I had a seven-year monogamous relationship with my lover. There's nothing about having AIDS which I feel that I should apologize for." Repentance does not mean asking forgiveness for being gay—but making peace with whatever your conscience sees as your mistakes.

Some PWAs do have a deep sense of remorse about the behavior that they believe exposed them to the HIV-virus. This feeling in some cases is rooted in self-hatred about being gay. Shame about one's sexuality only interferes with the self-acceptance which healing requires. Other people *are* bothered by a sexual life in their past which was rather indiscriminate, unsatisfying and very hard to control. These feelings need to be accepted in a spirit of forgiveness—not dismissed as puritanical, socialized guilt.

Because some people in our society see AIDS as God's punishment for homosexuality, I hesitate to mention Swamiji's thoughts about repentance. The last thing a person with AIDS needs is to be told he should be ashamed of himself. But a "searching and fearless moral inventory," as it is called in the twelve steps of Alcoholics Anonymous, is necessary for healing.

Look at your life. What do you feel were your mistakes? How have you failed to receive the gift of life? Failed in your responsibilities to yourself and others? And, most importantly, can you forgive yourself for these mistakes? Our hearts are healed as we learn to forgive and accept ourselves.

Stage Two: A clear resolve to stop doing things that damage or endanger your health, to block any further wastage of your immunity or energy

In yoga teaching there is a term, *prana*, which refers to the life force in an individual. It's similar to the term in Chinese medicine, *chi*. The French have the expression *elan vital*. No English word completely captures the concept of a life force or vitality which is crucial to promoting health and fighting off disease. We have a great deal of influence over the *prana* or energy level in our bodies. Very often we live or think in ways which deplete our *prana* or energy. So the second step in this self-generated healing process is the clear resolve to stop doing that which diminishes health or immunity or energy. Swami Satchidananda says:

> We have placed ourselves in a situation where we seem to have lost much of our inner strength, inner resistance. Immunity is based on the inner vital energy. We have to do two things. The first thing is to find out what caused the deficiency. What did we do? How did our life style take away our immunity? There are many, many reasons. Even by overeating you are overburdening your system. Everything in excess takes away our strength. Even a vehicle, if overloaded, won't pull you anymore. The engine will get heated. The head will blow out. We see that even in machines. The human body is

> a machine. So it's our duty first of all to find out what I did as an individual to lose my energy, lose my immunity. And immediately put a stop there. No more. Get back to the very natural lifestyle. Everything should be clean. Yes, from our thoughts to our food. Even wrong thinking. The major philosophy of homeopathy is based on this principle. Dr. Hahnemann, who invented the homeopathy system, brings this as the primary cause for disease.... that wrong thoughts, disturbing thoughts, poison the system. The same thing is true in Eastern thought, in the Ayurvedic system.

Homeopathy is a system of medicine based on the principle that *like cures like*. In other words, "substances that cause symptoms when given in large doses can cure illnesses with similar symptoms when given in microdoses."[1] Homeopathic doctors use microdoses of a single remedy chosen after looking at the entire picture of a patient. Dr. Andre Godfirnon, a homeopathic doctor in Los Angeles, reports that a homeopathic remedy developed by Doctors Janaer and Marichal in Brussels has been effective in arresting immune function deterioration in people with AIDS. These findings are based on studies with 60 patients in Africa. Even if you do not choose to take the homeopathic remedy specified for AIDS, you might consider trying homeopathic remedies for specific symptoms, instead of conventional medications which can cause serious side effects.

Swami Satchidananda continues:

> I always used to tell this in a sort of joking way. Every country has an entry point where foreigners come. When you arrive from a foreign flight, you just can't go in directly. You have to go first to the immigration, show your passport, visa, then customs checking. What's the reason? The authorities don't want any undesirable elements to be brought

into the country. So they check. Who are you? Where's your passport? Did you get a visa? What kind of philosophy do you follow? All these questions are asked.

In the same way, our body is our country. The Hindu scriptures call it the City of Nine Gates. It is a city with nine openings. You can count if you want. And things get through, into the city, through all those gates. Eyes, nose, mouth, ears and so on. And there are immigration officers at all entry points. Suppose you pick up a fruit. First you see it. "Ah, looks good. Bitten by any insects or anything?" You look around, using the eyes. These inspectors pass. "Okay, they are good. No problem." Then you bring it closer. Another inspector sniffs it. If there is a foul smell, he'll say, "Ah, throw it out. Go back to your country." But suppose this inspector also okays it. Then another important inspector takes one bite. If he also allows, then you swallow. See, there are three immigration officers here. And we are very clever. We can cheat all these three people. Wax your apple to look nice. Color your carrots. It cheats the inspectors. Put some nice scent and you cheat one man. You put on some sugar and you cheat another inspector. But the final authority is the one who takes it, the federal government—here. [He points to his stomach.]

Prana is the vital energy. It can always rebuild. It's never too late. That's what I want to tell the people with AIDS, whatever level they are at. The doctors may say it's advanced. But I really believe in a super-doctor—cosmic energy, the supreme authority who gives us prana.

Diet

What you eat affects your health as well as your state of mind. Abbey Semel, M.S., R.D., a nutritionist, makes the following recommendations based on her extensive experience working with HIV-positive people:

> The goal is a diet that boosts the immune system and is less stressful for the body. Just as our environment and our lifestyle can cause stress, a diet can stress the body. What I recommend is fairly basic—a *whole foods* diet: whole grains, fresh fruits and vegetables, low-fat high-fibre foods, and very low quantities of animal foods. Avoid animal foods because they are high in fat and are treated with chemicals, antibiotics, hormones and steroids. Avoid processed refined foods that are high in white flour, sugar and hydrogenated oils. Excess sugar stresses the body because it weakens the adrenal glands and depletes B-vitamins.
>
> We can get enough protein without eating animal products. There are eight amino acids which our body can not synthesize. When certain grains and beans are combined, one makes up the amino acids that the other is deficient in, and the result forms a complementary protein. For example, rice and beans provide complete protein. These complementary foods need not be eaten at the same meal in order to have the complementary effect, but should be eaten in the same day.
>
> Look at your basic relationship with food. Many people abuse food, eating for oblivion rather than health. Don't eat on the run. I don't think you absorb the nutrients if you eat as you are crossing a Manhattan street. Take a moment and be calm when you eat. Eat slowly. If you have a problem eating too fast, change hands. If you're right-

handed, eat with your left hand. Put your fork down between bites. Notice the smells and the textures and the flavors of the food. It's not something to be done unconsciously and without consideration of what the body needs for optimal health. Enjoy it. Take time to be thankful for the food. Be adventurous. Try foods you've never eaten before. Eating can promote health, boost your immune system and still be tasty. Food can be a great source of pleasure in your life.

People will only eat foods which they find tasty. Learn how to make delicious meals with whole foods. (A few references for whole foods cook books are contained in the bibliography at the end of this book.) Learn how to fit foods into your lifestyle and how to prepare food without taking a lot of time. Eat during the day, not at the end of the day when your body is less active. Some people do better with small amounts of food through the day rather than one or two large meals.

Don't make changes in your diet which are too radical and which do not appeal to you. Some people come in wanting to switch to a raw foods diet or a macrobiotic diet and get very discouraged when they are unable to follow it. *Think about the diet that you will be comfortable with. Then work step by step in that direction.*

You may resist these changes in your diet. Many people are willing to change every aspect of their lifestyle except their food. They don't want to take the time to make changes. It's easier to take a pill. When you feel well you are less motivated to make changes to promote your health. This is a common problem with people that are asymptomatic seropositives. Preventive medicine is often foreign to western medicine. I see food as preventive medicine. People would never put water in the gas tank of their car, but they neglect the needs of their bodies in ways which are similar to that kind of negligence in caring for their car.

Have variety in your diet. Some people think that the only grain to eat is wheat, but there are other grain sources. Food allergies are common; for example, allergies to wheat or milk products. By having a variety of foods, you are less likely to develop these allergies. It is not uncommon for HIV-positive people to experience candidiasis. For those people I recommend a yeast-free diet— excluding bread, baked products, cheese, vinegar, alcohol, anything that is fermented.

Eating out can be difficult. I don't recommend going to fast food restaurants because many of the foods are fried and refried in the same rancid oil. However, many restaurants are happy to prepare foods according to your taste—for example, serving salads with the dressing on the side, or grilling and steaming foods rather than frying them. Fresh juices are very healthy. They're a great way to get nutrients.

I always talk about exercise when I talk about food. Exercise is as important as your diet. Come up with an exercise program that you will enjoy—not one that is a burden, but one that is a source of pleasure. It needs to be convenient and affordable. I recommend 20-30 minutes three times a week, preferably continuous aerobic exercise. Walking is a good form of exercise. Remember to warm up and cool down for five to ten minutes before and after each period of exercise. During this time, breathe and stretch and relax your muscles. Stress gets

> stored in the muscles. Exercise helps to relieve that stress, and through that you get a new outlook on life.

Swami Satchidananda recommends avoiding caffeine and alcohol entirely. He believes that even small amounts can disturb the system of someone trying to build immunity. Tune in to your inner guide and sense what food you should eat. Pay attention not only to what you eat, but how much and with what attitude. In the Tibetan Buddhist tradition only very senior monks were allowed to prepare the food. It was a job only for sensitive, spiritually developed people. The importance of the attitude with which food is prepared is emphasized in many other traditions as well. It is not healthy to overeat, even if you are eating food which you consider nutritious. Swami Satchidananda is a proponent of vegetarianism:

> Let your food be clean. When I say clean, let it be the product of love. Let it not be the product of violence. A violent food will cause violence in the body. You can get plenty of protein with a vegetarian diet. Our bodies are vegetarian bodies. Compare your body—the tongue, the teeth, the eyes, the nails—to those of other animals. They are vegetarian animals. Our intestine is 22 feet long. A carnivorous animal has only four feet long. They have claws to run and catch prey. They have rough tongues to lick the flesh from the bone. Animal food doesn't come in a loving way to us. Every animal when you kill it goes through a trauma. It's afraid. Do you think the animal will die happily, lovingly? So even if the documents say that it's a healthy animal, at the time of the killing the meat becomes totally unhealthy. You cannot avoid that. I recommend clean vegetarian food. And with that, simple vegetables. Not with too much spice.

❖

Many other things can weaken our energy—the constant sensory stimulation of living in a city, having a television or a stereo on all day, living in a messy home, or participating in relationships which are draining. Think about how certain people affect your energy level. A lot of energy can go into the pursuit of a sexual experience. The yogic teachings state that a great deal of prana is expended in ejaculation. Many people waste a lot of energy with their sexual preoccupations. What is being emphasized here is the importance of looking at your entire life—behavior, food, stress level, intimate relationships, sexual expression—and determining ways in which your energy is lessened by your life style. What is problematic for one person may not be problematic for another.

If you are aware of ways in which your life is imbalanced, or ways in which you drain your energy, make a plan to change. What is important is that you undertake any plans for behavior or change with a winning mentality. In other words, approach the task—whether it's worrying less or eating less sugar—in a way in which you can succeed.

Stage Three: Building Immunity. Through healthful practices and positive constructive thoughts, the immune system is strengthened

Stage Two involved stopping ways in which you drain your energy. Stage Three consists of practices that build up your vitality or immunity. Resolve to do everything in your power to add more immunity to your system through clean diet, clean thoughts, and a lifestyle which you feel totally comfortable with. Feel that you are building your immunity on a daily basis. Rather than block your receptivity through thoughts and actions, make yourself open to this healing force. As Swami Satchidananda says, "Something cannot draw or conduct energy without being a clean channel."

For HIV-positive people who show symptoms of viral

activity, Swami Satchidananda recommends three hours of yoga practice each day. This becomes quite possible if you meditate for 45 minutes in the morning and evening, have one 60 minute hatha yoga session each day, and two visualizations of 15 minutes each. It takes discipline, but soon these practices become a habit. Without setting aside time several times a day, it's very difficult to develop a powerful healing vibration in your life. If you do these yoga practices regularly, they will help make daily life extremely satisfying.

Hatha Yoga

Hatha yoga is the physical aspect of yoga. When people speak of going to a yoga class, for example, they are almost always referring to hatha yoga. It includes the physical postures, deep relaxation and breathing practices. Examples of these postures, or *asanas* in Sanskrit, are forward bends, backward bends, shoulder stand, head stand, etc. They are best learned in a class, but can be learned with an audio tape, video tape or book. (Information is available in the directory in the back of this book.) Begin the practice easily and slowly. The physical postures precede a complete deep relaxation and then the yoga breathing exercises. When the breath slows down, then we are able to control the mind. We begin with the body, going from the gross to the subtle. You train the body and through the body you are training the mind.

Swami Satchidananda says:

> People say "I want to go directly to meditation." You are trying to go directly to the subtle part, which is very difficult to handle. The truth is, it is the subtle movement that causes the gross movement. But when you want control, you begin the other way. An example is starting a car. You turn the key. A spark causes the pistons to move. Then the connecting rods move the crank shaft, causing the fly wheel to rotate. Next, the gear box moves, causing the running shaft to rotate. The running

> shaft is connected with the differential, and finally, the axles turn the wheel. From the pistons, we slowly go to the wheel. Only then does the car move. When you decide you want to stop the car, you don't apply the brake at the pistons. You apply the brake at the very gross movement, the wheel. Then the action is reversed, and slowly everything stops. Likewise, our movement starts with the mind—the spark. It slowly develops into physical action. When you want to control the mind, begin by controlling the physical, the body. Then slowly, slowly, slowly go back to the mind.

The healing process recommended here includes the body. Exercise is very important and improves immune functioning. Yoga practices should be done *in addition* to other exercise, because they bring a relaxed vitality not available from only doing aerobic exercise.

Yoga Breathing Exercises

Swami Satchidananda explains the benefits of yoga:

> Our yoga postures tone the system. They can squeeze out the blockages, clear the way for putting in more prana. That's why we do the pranayama (breathing practices) after the asanas. I have total faith in pranayama. All you have to do is take a deep breath in. It's the cheapest and the best.

> Yoga brings health. When good health comes, ill health goes. And one of the most important practices to do is pranayama. In pranayama you are literally drinking gallons and gallons and gallons of vitality. Prana means vitality through the breath. That's the best tonic, and it's free; you don't have to buy it. That builds up your confidence, your physical and mental strength.

The purpose behind pranayama is to regulate the prana within. The question might arise, "Why do we want to control it? What is the use? Why not just let it move around?" But we are surrounded by pranic movements all the time. Everything outside of us moves, and we are continually bombarded by these movements and influenced by them. The environment, the people around us influence us; the air, the water, the sun, the moon, the stars—all these influence us. We cannot escape from that; so how can we make use of those influences for our benefit? We can't change outside influences, but we can change something within—by fortifying ourselves, by strengthening ourselves to handle them.

With Yoga you can develop immunity. By proper breathing you can charge your system with vitality and become immune to any disease. You don't have to fall into the clutches of "influenza" unless you allow it to "influence" you. A good yogi need not be afraid of anything.

The Lord created you. He didn't create you just to be frightened by all these little, even invisible germs, which the doctors say frighten us more than even the visible enemies. Every cell of your system can be fortified. Let every cell be a soldier in your system. We have a great battalion in us, a defensive system. God has given it to us: nature has built that into us.

The bloodstream gets contaminated by carbon from the different movements of the body. As the oxygen is drawn in, the carbon is thrown out. Thus, the oxygen takes away the carbon and purifies the blood. So in our normal breathing we get a certain amount of purification. But if we do deep yogic breathing, in addition to the purification of the blood, the extra oxygen goes into the system and every cell is oxygenated.

With proper pranayama you begin to expand your lungs completely. In a deep breath, you take in about seven times as much oxygen as in a normal breath. You supercharge the blood with extra oxygen. Oxygen is life; without oxygen there is no life. That means you are enriching your blood with a lot of life. Your red corpuscles become even redder. The quality of the blood improves.

Not only do you take in more oxygen, but, along with the air, you take in more prana. The oxygen gets diffused in the lungs and then gets into the bloodstream, but the prana goes all through the person. It enters your physical, vital, and mental areas. That's why with a deep breath you can send your prana to any part of the body you want. Every cell of your body vibrates with new life. At that point no viruses can even think of coming near you. As soon as they come near you they get burnt out, because you have charged your system with so much life force and built up your army within. Normally we are not living one hundred per cent; most of the cells are dying. If we really want to live, we must do the yogic breathing. That is the beauty of pranayama.

I once read an article about a baby who had blood poisoning. It was an emergency case, and they flew the baby to the hospital. They couldn't even treat the child because the poison was all through the body, so they decided to place him in a pressurized oxygen chamber. After a few hours they took him out and found that half the poison was gone. That is because oxygen is a great panacea, the best medicine for all kinds of poisons and viruses. It is life. That's why breathing is so very, very important. Even if you miss doing the asanas occasionally, don't miss the breathing practices. At least do a few deep breathings several times a day. Prana is the best tonic. Simple breathing can heal.

When you do the deep breathing feel that you are inhaling a lot of prana, a lot of vital energy. Hold your breath for a few seconds while thinking that the prana is going directly to the place that aches and that it is building it up by removing the dead or diseased cells and tension. Then, when you breathe out, feel that you are throwing out all of the illness. You can feel that with the inhaling breath fresh energy comes in, and with the exhaling breath the collected dirt is thrown out. By doing this, you can cure many of the aches and pains in the body, as well as long-standing illnesses. Prana has that power. It can penetrate anywhere and everywhere—just by your thinking.

Mantras and Affirmations

Another vital healing practice is consciously affirming positive thoughts. Examples of affirmations are: "I am putting in more immunity. I am healthy in body and mind." Or "I am the true spirit, independent of the body and mind, which is disease-free." People can do affirmations for any goal, including health or spiritual development. When done regularly, the practitioner often finds dramatic results. Nevertheless, people often have resistance to doing affirmations regularly. Louise Hay reminds people that if it were easy, if they totally believed the affirmation, they wouldn't have to do it in the first place. The idea is to educate not only the conscious and subconscious minds, but all the cells of the body. I would recommend setting aside specific periods to affirm thoughts of health and peace of mind. These are done best at the end of a deep relaxation, when the body and mind are relaxed. Somewhat similar to affirmations is mantra repetition.

Changing the thought forms is the basis of the healing process. You want to bring better vibrations into the system. Mantras are very helpful for his purpose. In Swamiji's words:

> What is a mantra? The very meaning of mantra is anything that steadies your mind. Man-tra. "Man" is mind, "tra" is the one who makes it steady. That's all. They are certain sound vibrations. God is nothing but word. God and word are one and the same. What is word? It's a mantra. Sound vibrations. Modern science also proves that everything ultimately is sound vibrations. The entire creation is the product of sound vibrations. You can charge everything with sound vibrations. So saying the proper mantras can realign the molecules, the hormones, repair the body.
>
> Now the question is what mantra? If it was my product I could sell it to you, but it's not mine, it's nature's. There are many, not just one or two. Simply repeat Hari Om. It's not a Hindu god or a Sanskrit god. It's mainly done for its vibrations. Hari Om. Keep repeating. Let the whole body, every cell, vibrate in that sound. A great saint said, "Even when I forget it, my cells repeat it." That's the power of mantra. Om Shanti, Hari Om. Any holy name, it doesn't matter. Do it with full faith in it, total confidence. That's important. And repeat, repeat, repeat until you hear that yourself, without even your repeating your body and mind should be repeating. At night, when all of a sudden you wake up, you'll be surprised that something is repeating the mantra in you. The power of that repetition.
>
> Let your selected mantra be thought again and again and again. Keep repeating. In the beginning

you have to do it. After some time your cells take over. Like any other practice, in the beginning *you* have to be conscious of the keyboard when you play the piano. You have to be conscious of the bow when you play the violin. You have to be conscious of your pedal and brake when you bicycle. Afterwards you don't even think of it. You simply go. And practice becomes firm if it's done for a long time without break, with total faith. We have to fulfill all these three qualities. Don't blame your mantra if you don't fulfill these qualities. Mantra can really work wonders. It can completely change your cells, repair all the cells, burn out all the undesirable decayed cells and build the new ones. No doubt about it. The world is yet to know the power of mantra.

Sometimes people come here and think, "What is chanting? What kind of howling is that?" They don't even understand. "Are they trying to convert us to be Hindus?" How can such suspicions come? Because they don't really understand what is its purpose—the scientific reason behind. Chanting is not just praying to some god, no. You don't have to have faith in God at all. Because your chanting itself produces certain vibrations. Sound vibrations. And if you chant the right words, you produce the right vibrations.

Remember, sound vibrations can do great things to us. Haven't you heard or seen watches and jewels that are cleaned with sound vibrations? Ultrasonic. What does it mean? Sound can clean up things. It can clean and it can put in fresh energy. Chant any nice holy names, sacred names. If you don't believe in the holy names, it's okay. You can say Om. Even if Om belongs to Buddhists and Hindus, forget that. We put labels: "Oh that belongs to me not you.

> Amen is mine, Om is yours." We have grabbed the land and put marks here and there. This is my land, that's your land.... Even God has not escaped that. "Jesus, my name. We follow Jesus. You follow Moses." And the Moses people, "We don't like to even say Jesus." And Jesus and Moses are condemned by the Krishna people. "Krishna is the only one." Another one: "Krishna, Jesus, Moses—Allah is the best." Another will condemn everything and say, "Supreme Brahman, Brahman." This kind of fight is going on and on and we have killed enough people. Let's not worry about all those people who try to grab things and put their label on it. Everything belongs to everybody. Know that. The entire world belongs to us. The entire cosmos belongs to us. We are all proper, legal inheritants, heirs to that. Nobody can just put a label and say, "This is mine."
>
> Repeat any sound that can produce lots of vibrations. Let the whole body vibrate. You are producing an ultrasonic sound in your own system. Sit there and do it every morning, noon, and evening. Half hour, 15 minutes. Om Shanti, Om Shanti. Shanti means peace. It's everybody's. So, that sound vibration is very important. Hari Om. We chant Hari Om. Hari Om is a great chant. It brings out all your energy.

Your Home as a Healing Environment

Another important suggestion is to create a healing environment within your own home. As Swami Satchidananda says:

> If you live in a room and you are thinking something constantly, the room gets charged with those thought forms. That's your room. It's a body outside the body. Society is formed that way with collective thoughts. Your room should be clean and pleasant,

with good vibrations. It shouldn't look like a junk yard. However sick you are, keep a few things and keep them neat. All these things help to heal.

Silence

Periods of silence are also very beneficial. If you can experience two hours a day with no music, no television, no conversation—simply silent—you'll find your whole system calming down beautifully. Study of spiritual books is acceptable as you begin the period of silence. Swami Satchidananda says, "Real truth is expressed by silence and understood by silence, not by the mind." When you are in your most upset state of mind, try to sit still. Just sit in silence and relax without much sensory stimulation. You will find a peacefulness coming from within you.

Laughter

Laughter is another important part of the natural healing process. Swamiji says:

> Laughter is the best remedy. You all know Norman Cousins' story. Daily, even if there's nobody else there, laugh. It doesn't matter. Your roommate or somebody else might think you're crazy, don't worry. Simply stand in front of the wall and laugh. Hearty, healthy, happy laughter. It will make you feel better, much better.

Additional Practices

Swami Satchidananda at different times has made other specific recommendations for AIDS-related difficulties. Although they might sound strange to many Americans, if you feel inclined, try one of these methods. See if they are effective for you. For everyone, he recommends saunas or steam baths to open the pores and eliminate toxins. For people with respiratory problems, he recommends extended periods of yoga breathing practices or pranayama. For those with lymph node swellings, he recommends fasting for a couple of days if possible, a juice fast is okay, and while fasting, taking an enema each day. For anyone experiencing skin inflammations, he recommends mud packs, which can be done with clay or with mud found alongside a stream. Cover your body up to the neck with mud and sit in the shade for 20-30 minutes. Then wash the body off thoroughly. Swamiji says:

> Mud is a great source. It can suck out all the poisons. I've tried it myself. Any inflammation, simply put on a mud pack. Mahatma Gandhi was a great believer in this. He treated his own son, who had small pox. I treated my son the same way when he had small pox. My relatives were cursing me, but afterwards, after the mud pack treatment he didn't have any scars. I believe in natural cures. I've worked with good capable people in the field and seen many healings.

Stage Four: Fearlessness

Never give up. As Michael Callen says:

> I have become convinced as a result of my own experience with AIDS and from my interviews with about 25 other long-term survivors that there is a bi-directional, mind-body connection which some day we may be able to pin down scientifically. I think the body needs to receive a "live" message. The mind needs to tell the body to fight, that life is precious and worth living. The mind is a great, largely untapped pharmacy. And we've got to find creative ways to mine it. Joy juice is what the body needs to live. And hope is like the air that we breathe. Without it we wither and die.[2]

Luis Palacios-Jimenez says:

> Hope helped me realize that I AM NOT

> DOOMED. When we concede to fear and hopelessness, we are in fact doomed. When we insist on living and surviving, and we do what we can to heal both the living body and the spirit we are not doomed.[3]
>
> Stop praying for miracles! You have everything you need to cope with this *inside of you*. There's a touch of God in all of us if you're willing to find him/her. This is truly the miracle.[4]

One member of a seminar said, "What helped me is realizing that fear is something I created. Fear is always something that is *going* to happen. Fear does not really exist. It's electricity, it goes through your brain. We have control over that."

When fears become overwhelming, it is best to share these feelings with others. Another group member spoke of being very frightened and panicked when he was hospitalized. He said that he did not expect that his parents and other family members would be understanding. In his desperation, he told them what he was feeling and, to his surprise, they were extremely understanding. By letting your fears and tears come out, you are in a much more effective position to approach healing.

Stage Five: Faith in a higher power

The notion of a higher power or a vaster awareness is very important in the healing process. This idea might put off those with a secular understanding of life. People who enter Alcoholics Anonymous sometimes are opposed to the spiritual dimension of the program, which states that surrender to a higher power is essential in maintaining sobriety. Some want to reject that part of the program and are counseled to act *as if* there were a higher power in their lives. This means to approach life as an experiment in which you assume that there is a spiritual reality or Higher Power which can guide your life. Often "acting as if" leads to a deeper more authentic faith.

Reverend Margaret Fuller, who leads a prayer ministry, says that if we do things in the name of God, "It's not our glory if healing does happen, and it's not our failure if it does not happen." Faith goes against the mind's rational perspective. A friend went to her spiritual teacher and said that she was ready for a deeper experience but needed a push off the diving board. The teacher replied that no one could push someone else off the diving board, that she would have to do that on her own initiative.

Swami Satchidananda offers an understanding of faith in a higher power.

> Peace is the nature of God. I see God as peace. God has no form. He has no other name. He is all peaceful. He is all serenity. That peace is to be felt. It is to be experienced within oneself. Peace and joy are our goal. The real God, the absolute God, the cosmic God, who is being searched for by one and all, is that peace and joy. When you are in peace, you are with God. Nothing from outside can give you peace. Because peace is there within you. When you disturb your peace, you are denying the God within you. Let us know that there is a vast ocean of consciousness which we call God.
>
> Become humble and selfless. Then you will get a glimpse of God's joy. Whatever change you want to happen outside should happen within. Your first duty is to find that peace within.
>
> Difficult situations may come. They give us a chance to prove our faith in a higher energy. The entire nature is the omnipresent guru. Draw silent lessons from all around you. Forget the past, don't worry about the future, live in the golden present.

Let us realize that this higher energy is taking care of everything. Trust wholeheartedly. You are putting yourself in the hands of a greater doctor, in the hands of a higher force. Listen to it as it guides you from within.

The Process of Self-Generated Healing

A Daily Journal

A daily journal provides insight into your healing journey. In the front of your notebook, you might find it useful to list ways in which you drain your energy as well as ways you promote your healing. Keep the notebook with you throughout the day and write down whatever comes to mind.

In your daily journal, you might want to make note of the following:

- each day's significant events and feelings
- all food eaten (including beverages)
- meditation
- exercise and Hatha yoga
- all medicine taken/any medical symptoms
- list relevant events which are health-promoting (e.g. massage, support group) or health-impairing (e.g unsafe sex, lack of sleep)

Establish a plan for self-generated healing. This should include daily practices. Do not make a plan which is too difficult to follow. Before making the plan consider how your behavior in the following areas is affecting your health: sexual behavior, diet, drugs/alcohol, meditation, exercise and Hatha yoga. The plan should include guidelines for whatever areas most need attention. Go over your plan with a friend or counselor—someone whose support you value. One person, for example, might exercise regularly, eat well, but drink too much wine and have unsafe sex. Another may need to focus on daily meditation and eating a more wholesome diet. Make a simple plan which is within your grasp. After each month, review and make whatever revisions would be most helpful.

> Problems help us develop our inner resources. Even in the intensity, enjoy yourself. Be playful and relaxed. You need adversity to know the truth. Always remember your goal. The goal is to realize your true nature, your peace, your happiness, your godliness. If you understand the goal, and you dedicate yourself to achieving it, you won't get disheartened by failures. Every failure must be a stepping stone for your further success. Use all the failures as stepping stones—one after another. Then they are all helping experiences. Your very interest in attaining your goal will take you to it. Your spiritual practices are the master key to open everything—health, wealth, strength. All of your practices can be joyful celebrations. So take it easy, but don't be lazy. It is very important to find the golden medium. Go to your capacity, but never overdo. Growth is natural, not painful. Remember, the pure self does not have to become happy. It is happiness itself. Your practices are not done to bring you happiness or peace, but to prevent the peace that is your true nature from being disturbed.
>
> Everything worthwhile takes its own time. If you attempt perfection in one day, you are not going to achieve much of anything. This applies particularly to developing the spiritual force. Begin with little things daily and one day you will be doing things that months before you thought impossible.
>
> —Swami Satchidananda

As has every other epidemic, AIDS will end some day—we hope, before too long. At an enormous price, life is much less frivolous. AIDS has reminded us that our lives can end much sooner and far more painfully than we had expected. AIDS is an epidemic that challenges us to explore the power and wisdom in our hearts. May we continue that journey long after the AIDS crisis has passed.

❖

Appendix

Hatha Yoga: Introduction and Explanation

❖

An audio-cassette of a hatha yoga class, taught by Prema Pleva, is available with this book. A few recommendations about listening to that cassette or going to a yoga class might be helpful.

The purpose of hatha yoga is to completely relax, tone and revitalize the entire system, and to help you control and relax the mind. A central part of hatha yoga is the bodily postures, called *asanas*. These are not "exercises"—which usually require quick movement and involve a measure of strain. *Asana* means steady, comfortable pose. Your body is different each day. A pose which you did easily on Monday may be very difficult on Tuesday. Be gentle with your body. The poses should not be painful. Wear loose clothes and do not eat for three hours before the class. Remove watches, glasses and jewelry.

The yoga class is a moving meditation. The benefits of yoga are directly proportional to the quality of awareness you bring to the experience. Make a resolve to leave your problems outside the room. Remain focused on what is happening in your body and mind in the present moment. If you are looking for a yoga class in your neighborhood, find one which peaceful. Some classes today overemphasize exercise and lack a meditative dimension. When you are in the class, try not to compete with others. Make the class a very personal experience.

The Integral Yoga hatha class follows an established pattern. After a few minutes of chanting and eye exercises, the class continues with the sun worship. The sun worship is a series of 12 positions which limber up the body for the rest of the class. Next are three backward bending poses: cobra, locust and bow. These are followed by forward bending poses—the half- and full-forward bends. The shoulder stand follows, which is complemented by the fish pose. After the half-spinal twist, you will be doing yoga mudra, which is the final asana. The diagram which follows will be helpful in giving you a visual picture of the class.

After the asanas, the class continues with a deep relaxation and *pranayama*, or yogic breathing. These are vital parts of the class which should always be included. If your time is limited, reduce the time you spend doing asanas, but always include deep relaxation and pranayama. The Integral Yoga hatha class ends with a brief silent meditation and a prayer or affirmation calling for peace and spiritual realization.

INTEGRAL YOGA HATHA CLASS SHEET

Resources

❖

National Hotlines

National AIDS Hotline: 1-800-342-7512 (24 hrs, for information and referral to local AIDS service organizations in the US. (Amer. Social Health Assoc.)

AIDS Crisisline: 1-800-221-7044 (for info/referral nationwide); in NY: 212-529-1604. (National Gay & Lesbian Task Force).

For information on government sponsored drug trials: 1-800-TRIALS-A.

Newsletters

PWA Coalition Newsline, 31 W. 26th Street, New York, NY 10010. 212-532-0290.

Treatment Issues, GMHC Department of Medical Information, 129 W. 20th St., New York, NY 1011 (free).

AIDS Treatment News, John H. James, PO Box 411256, San Francisco, CA 94141 (biweekly).

Bulletin of AIDS Treatment Information (BETA), San Francisco AIDS Foundation. 415-863-AIDS.

PI Perspectives, Project Inform, 347 Delores St., Ste. 301, San Francisco, CA 94110. 1-800-822-7422.

Body Positive, 2095 Broadway, Suite 306, New York, NY 10023. 212-633-1782.

Glossary

❖

AIDS (Acquired Immune Deficiency Syndrome): a virus-caused disease that results in a breakdown of the pattern of immune protection called cell-mediated immunity. The individual is left vulnerable to a host of bacterial, viral, fungal and protozoic invasions.

ARC (AIDS-related complex): an acquired syndrome resembling AIDS but lacking the presence of the serious opportunistic infections which are required for an AIDS diagnosis. Persons with ARC often have chronic symptoms such as lymph node enlargement, fever, diarrhea, lethargy, and localized infections.

antibody: a protein formed by lymphocytes that has the capacity to react against certain foreign substances.

asymptomatic: having no symptoms of disease.

azidothymidine (AZT): an experimental antiviral drug which research has shown is associated with delay of AIDS symptoms in HIV-infected individuals.

Candida albicans: a fungus that is a part of the normal flora of the mucous membranes in the respiratory, gastrointestinal, and female genital tracts. In immunocompromised persons, it may gain dominance, producing pathological conditions and may be associated with severe systemic disease.

candidiasis: a condition produced by infection with Candida albicans, capable of involving a wide range of tissues of the body, including the skin, mucous membranes, nails, bronchi, lungs, heart, vagina, gastrointestinal tract, brain, and bloodstream.[1]

Centers for Disease Control: a federal agency located in Atlanta, Georgia, that plans, conducts, coordinates, and evaluates national programs for the prevention and control of transmissible diseases and other preventable conditions.[2]

Cryptosporidium: a class of protozoa, containing several types capable of being opportunistic and producing severe inflammation of the small intestine and colon in compromised hosts.[3]

Cryptococcus neoformans: a fungus that may infect the skin, lungs, or bones, which has a predilection for the central nervous system, causing primarily meningitis. In the severely immunocompromised host, it may disseminate via the bloodstream to any site in the body.[4]

cytomegalovirus: a virus capable of being opportunistic and causing disseminated disease in immunocompromised hosts.[5]

Epstein-Barr virus: a virus that is the cause of infectious mononucleosis and that has been suggested as capable of causing other diseases in immunocompromised hosts.[6]

generalized lymphadenopathy syndrome: a syndrome of enlargement of lymph nodes seen in increasing frequency in risk groups for AIDS, and thought to represent a condition related to infection with the AIDS virus.[7]

helper T cells (T4 cells): thymus-derived lymphocytes which stimulate antibody production. The HIV virus is believed to damage the immune system by infecting the helper T cells.

herpes zoster: an acute disease, also called shingles, characterized by painful eruptions on the skin or mucous membranes.

HIV: Human Immunodeficiency Virus. The virus believed to cause AIDS.

HIV positive: the term used to describe those whose blood tests have shown antibodies to the HIV virus.

immune system: a combination of cells and proteins that assist the host organism's ability to fight foreign substances, including microorganisms such as viruses and bacteria.[8]

Kaposi's sarcoma: a previously rare cancer primarily of the skin and lymph nodes that occurs frequently in those with AIDS. This cancer often manifests itself clinically as painless reddish-purple blotches on the skin. Its presence is regarded as evidence of AIDS even in the absence of an opportunistic infection.

lymph: a clear, transparent fluid collected from tissues throughout the body and flowing in special lymph vessels, eventually connecting and adding to the circulation of blood through the veins.

lymph node: small rounded bodies that produce lymphocytes to fight invading substances. They are defense posts for the body against foreign substances causing disease.

lymphadenopathy: lymph node enlargement. (See generalized lymphadenopathy syndrome).

lymphocyte: a type of white blood cell found in blood, lymph, and other specialized tissue such as bone marrow and tonsils. Two major classes, B- and T-lymphocytes, are crucial components of the immune system. The B-lymphocytes are the cells primarily responsible for antibody production, while the T-lymphocytes are involved in the direct attack against invading organisms. A subtype of T-lymphocyte, the helper T- lymphocyte, is the main cell infected and destroyed by the AIDS virus.[9]

lymphoma: any tumor, usually malignant, of the lymphatic tissues.

meningitis: any inflammation of the membranes lining the spinal cord and brain.

MAI (Mycobacterium avium-intracellulare): a species of Mycobacteria, capable of causing severe lung disease in immunocompromised hosts.

PCP (Pneumocystis carinii pneumonia): a pneumonia caused by a protozoan found widely in nature, causing no disease in normal individuals, but causing debilitating disease, usually of the lungs, in immunocompromised persons.

PWA (person with AIDS).

seropositivity: synonymous with antibody positivity.

T-cell: lymphocytes which are transported from the bone marrow to the thymus gland. They are principally involved in the direct attack against invading organisms (see lymphocytes).

thrush: a fungal infection due to Candida albicans, characterized by small, whitish spots on the tongue and inner surface of the cheeks

Toxoplasma gondii: a protozoan widely found in nature, normally not disease-producing in healthy persons, but resulting in Toxoplasmosis, a devastating disease of the nervous system and eyes in immunocompromised hosts.[10]

vaccine: a preparation administered to induce long-term immunity against a particular agent.

virus: any of a vast group of minute infectious agents. They can grow and reproduce only within living host cells, which they do by invading the cell and taking over the workings of the cell itself. Viruses are capable of causing devastating disease in immunocompromised individuals, and are not affected by antibiotics.

References

❖

Part I

Introduction. Finding Hope in a Time of Crisis

1. William L. Heyward and James W. Curran, "The Epidemiology of AIDS in the U.S.," *Scientific American*, October 1988, pp. 72-81.

2. Jonathan M. Mann, James Chin, Peter Piot, and Thomas Quinn, "The International Epidemiology of AIDS," *Scientific American*, October 1988, pp. 82-89.

3. Statements in this book which are attributed to Dr. Michael Lerner were made during his talk at the Association for the Advancement of Behavior Therapy on November 19, 1988 in New York City. The title of his address was "The Effects of Residential Health-Promotion on Quality of Life for Cancer Patients."

4. The quotations of Swami Satchidananda contained in this book are from his public talks as well as from personal conversations I have had with him.

Chapter 1. Taking the Test

No notes.

Chapter 2. Facing HIV with Courage and Hope

1. Luis Palacios-Jiminez, "Little Bits of Wisdom," in *Surviving and Thriving with AIDS: Collected Wisdom Volume Two*, ed. Michael Callen (New York: PWA Coalition, 1988), p. 24.

2. Christopher D. Sherman, "My Suggestions for Those Diagnosed with AIDS," in *Surviving and Thriving with AIDS: Collected Wisdom Volume Two*, ed. Michael Callen, p. 16.

3. Christopher Spence, AIDS: *The Time to Reclaim Our Power*, (London publisher, not stated on manuscript, 1986) p. 4.

4. Stephen Bodian, "The Healing We Took Birth For," Yoga Journal, July/August 1987, p. 40.

5. Matt Clark with Karen Springer, Mary Hager, Lisa Drew, and Jeanne Gordon, "Cancer Hurts before it Kills," Newsweek, December 19, 1988.

6. Stephen Levine, *Who Dies?* (New York: Anchor Press/ Doubleday, 1982) pp. 114-115.

7. Al S. Fecouravicus and Michael W. Otto, "Managing Chronic Illness Behavior," a workshop presented by Association for Advancement of Behavior Therapy convention, New York City, November 18, 1988.

8. Michael Callen, "AIDS 201" in *Surviving & Thriving, Volume Two*, ed. Michael Callen, p.3.

9. Jean Claude Carriere, *The Mahabharata*, a play translated by Peter Brook (New York: Harper & Row, 1987), p. 105.

10. Quotations of Stephen Levine which are not cited in his books were made during his workshops.

Chapter 3. Caring for Someone with AIDS

1. Sister Patrice Murphy, "Pastoral Care and Persons with AIDS," *The American Journal of Hospice Care*, March/April 1986, p. 38.

2. Brenda Lukeman, *Embarkations: A Guide to Dealing with Death and Parting* (Englewood Cliffs, NJ: Spectrum/Prentice Hall, 1982), p. xiii.

3. Stephen Levine and Ram Dass, "Exploring the Heart of Healing," audio cassettes (Novato, California: The Access Group, 1988).

4. Jean Vanier, *Be Not Afraid* (Toronto: Paulist Press, 1975) p. viii.

5. Carl Rogers, *A Way of Being* (Boston: Houghton Mifflin, 1980), pp. 137-159.

6. Leston Havens, *Making Contact* (Cambridge, MA: Harvard University Press, 1986), p. 24.

7. Dr. Siegel frequently makes this point during his public lectures.

Part II

Introduction. Learning from Others

1. Viktor E. Frankl, *Man's Search for Meaning* (New York, Washington Square Press, 1985), p. 86.

Chapter 4. Facing the Challenge

1. Viktor Frankl, ibid. p. 47.

2. Steven Locke, M.D. and Douglas Corrigan, *The Healer Within: The New Medicine of Mind and Body* (New York: A Mentor Book/New American Library, 1986), p. 220.

3. Stephen Levine, *Healing Into Life and Death* (Garden City, NY: Anchor Press/Doubleday, 1987), p. 53.

4. Daniel Goleman, "The Mind Over the Body," *The New York Times Magazine*, September 27, 1987, p. 39.

5. Bernie S. Siegel, M.D., *Love, Medicine and Miracles* (New York: Harper & Row, 1986), p. 24.

6. Michael Callen, "I Will Survive," *Village Voice*, May 3, 1988, p. 31.

7. Michael Callen, ibid. pp. 34-35.

8. Dr. Simonton made this statement during a panel discussion at the New Jersey Metaphysical Society conference in October, 1988.

Chapter 5. The Mind/Body Connection

1. Locke and Corrigan, *The Healer Within*, p.10.

2. Siegel, *Love, Medicine & Miracles*, p. 2.

3. Locke and Corrigan, *The Healer Within*, p. 13.

4. Dr. Fauci made these statements at a talk at Bard College in Annandale-on-Hudson, NY on November 12, 1988. His lecture was titled "Current Issues and Future Directions in the Scientific Response to the AIDS Epidemic."

5. Callen, "I Will Survive," p. 35.

6. Callen, Ibid. p. 34.

7. *Newsweek*, November 7, 1988, p. 92.

8. Ibid.

9. Joan Borysenko, PhD., *Minding the Mind, Mending the Body* (Reading, MA: Addison Wesley, 1987), p. 12.

10. Norman Cousins, *Anatomy of an Illness as Perceived by the Patient* (New York: W.W. Norton & Co., 1979), pp. 155-6.

11. Jeanne Achterberg, *Imagery in Healing: Shamanism in Modern Medicine* (Boston: New Science Library/ Shambala, 1985) p. 169.

12. Ibid. p. 170.

13. Locke and Corrigan, *The Healer Within*, pp. 2-4.

14. Ibid. pp. 227-228.

15. The Oprah Winfrey Show, August 21, 1987.

16. Locke and Corrigan, *The Healer Within*, pp. 4-5.

17. Ibid. p. 18.

18. Siegel, *Love, Medicine & Miracles*, p. 25.

19. Locke and Corrigan, *The Healer Within*, pp. 171-2.

20. Ibid. p. 75.

21. Norman Cousins, *Anatomy of an Illness*, p. 79.

22. Steven James, "Reflections on Healing, Honesty and Personal Power," *Surviving and Thriving with AIDS: Hints for the Newly Diagnosed*, Michael Callen, Editor (New York: People with AIDS Coalition, 1987), pp. 35-36.

23. Dr. Siegel refers to study by Pennebaker in his public talks.

24. Siegel, *Love, Medicine & Miracles*, p. 187.

25. Achterberg, *Imagery in Healing*, p. 173.

26. Michael A. Weiner, Ph.D., *Maximum Immunity* (New York: Pocket Books/Simon & Schuster, 1986), pp. 14-15.

27. Locke & Corrigan, *The Healer Within*, pp. 103.

28. Jerome D. Frank, *Persuasion and Healing: A Comparative Study of Psychotherapy* (New York: Schochen Books, 1974), pp. 66-71.

29. Bernie Siegel, *Love, Medicine & Miracles*, pp. 51-52.

30. Locke and Corrigan, *The Healer Within*, p. 17.

31. Ibid. p. 84.

32. Ibid. p. 98.

33. Bernie Siegel, *Love, Medicine & Miracles*, p. 76.

34. Locke and Corrigan, *The Healer Within*, p. 101.

35. Ibid. pp. 81-82.

36. Ibid. pp. 23-25.

37. Ibid. pp. 77-79.

38. Joan Borysenko, *Minding the Mind, Mending the Body*, p. 21.

39. Bernie Siegel, *Love, Medicine & Miracles*, p. 72-73.

40. Locke and Corrigan, *The Healer Within*, p. 78.

41. Ibid. pp. 85-87.

42. Ibid. p. 71.

43. Michael A. Weiner, *Maximum Immunity*, p. 50.

44. Locke and Corrigan, *The Healer Within*, pp. 89-90.

45. Ibid. p. 105.

46. Bernie Siegel, *Love, Medicine & Miracles*, p. 29.

47. Ibid. p. 71.

48. Joan Borysenko, *Minding the Mind, Mending the Body*, p.

Chapter 6. Taking Charge of our Lives

1. Paul Lee, PhD., "The Vital Roots of Immunity," *Psychoimmunity & The Healing Process*, ed. Jason Serinus (Berkeley, CA: Celestial Arts, 1986), pp. 30-31.

2. Joan Borysenko, *Minding the Mind, Mending the Body*, p.23.

Chapter 7. Meditation

1. Herbert Benson, "The Relaxation Response: A Bridge Between Medicine & Religion," *The Harvard Medical School Mental Health Letter* (vol. 4, no. 9, March 1988), pp. 4-6.

2. Sri Swami Satchidananda, *Integral Yoga: The Yoga Sutras of Patanjali* (Pomfret Center, CT: Integral Yoga Publications, 1978).

3. Herbert Benson, "The Relaxation Response: A Bridge Between Medicine & Religion," pp. 5-6.

4. Ibid.

5. Joseph Goldstein and Jack Kornfeld, *Seeking the Heart of Wisdom: The Path of Insight Meditation* (Boston, MA: Shambala Publ., 1987), p. 7.

6. Henri J.M. Nouwen, *Behold the Beauty of the Lord: Praying with Icons* (Notre Dame, IN: Ave Maria Press, 1987), p. 22.

7. Ram Dass, *Journey of Awakening: A Meditator's Guidebook* (Toronto, Canada: Bantam Books, 1978), p. 2.

8. Herbert Benson, "The Relaxation Response: A Bridge

Between Medicine & Religion," p. 5.

9. Joseph Goldstein and Jack Kornfeld, *Seeking the Heart of Wisdom*, pp. 31-45.

10. Ram Dass, *Journey of Awakening*, p. 9.

11. Quoted in *Spiritual Diary* (Honesdale, PA: The Himalayan International Institute, 1978)

12. Joseph Goldstein and Jack Kornfeld, *Seeking the Heart of Wisdom*, p. 44.

Chapter 8. Imagery and Healing

1. Jeanne Achterberg, *Imagery in Healing: Shamanism and Modern Medicine* (Boston, MA: New Science Library/ Shambala, 1985), p. 11.

2. Adelaide Bry, *Visualization: Directing the Movies of Your Mind* (New York: Barnes & Noble Books/Harper & Row, 1976), p. 13.

3. Arnold Lazarus, Ph.D., *In the Mind's Eye: The Power of Imagery for Personal Enrichment* (New York: The Guilford Press, 1985), pp. 53-74.

4. *New York Times*, May 23, 1988.

5. Martin L. Rossman, MD, *Healing Yourself: A Step by Step Program for Better Health Through Imagery* (New York, Walker Publishing Co., 1987), pp. 14-27.

6. Louise L. Hay, *You Can Heal Your Life* (Farmingdale, NY: Coleman Publ., 1984), p. 12.

7. Francis MacNutt, o.p., *The Power to Heal* (Notre Dame, IN: Ave Maria Press, 1977), p. 39.

8. Barbara Leahy Shlemon, *Healing Prayer* (Notre Dame, IN: Ave Maria Press, 1976), pp. 48-49.

9. Martin L. Rossman, *Healing Yourself*, p. 71.

10. The imagery exercises in this chapter are influenced by the work of Jeanne Achterberg, Martin L. Rossman, Stephen Levine, and Swami Satchidananda.

11. Arnold Lazarus, *In the Mind's Eye*, pp. 21-23.

Chapter 9. The Power of Our Thoughts

1. Piero Ferrucci, *What We May Be* (Los Angeles: Jeremy Tarcher, Inc., distributed by St. Martin's Press, NY, 1982), pp. 48-49.

2. Ibid. p. 49.

3. Richard F. Rakos, PhD and Harold E. Schroeder, PhD, *Participant's Manual: Self-Directed Assertiveness Training* (New York: BMA Audio Cassettes Program, a Division of Guilford Publishers, 1980), p. 26.

4. Patricia Carrington, PhD, *Releasing* (New York: William Morrow, 1984), pp. 46-49.

Chapter 10. The Stages of Self-Generated Healing

1. Richard Leviton, "Homeopathy," in *Yoga Journal*, March/April 1989, issue 85, p. 45.

2. Michael Callen, "AIDS 201," in *Surviving and Thriving with AIDS: Collected Wisdom*, volume two, ed. Michael Callen, p. 2.

3. Luis Palacios-Jiminez, "Hope - Excerpts From a Sermon Delivered to Integrity New York" in *Surviving and Thriving with AIDS: Collected Wisdom*, volume two, ed. Michael Callen, p. 18.

4. Luis Palacios-Jiminez, "Little Bits of Wisdom," in *Surviving and Thriving with AIDS: Collected Wisdom*, volume two, ed. Michael Callen, p. 24.

Glossary

1. Frumkin, Lyn, M.D. and McGrath, Michael S., M.D., *Questions and Answers in AIDS*, New York: Avon Books, 1987, p. 140.

2. Ibid.

3. Ibid. p. 141

4. bid.

5. Ibid.

6. Ibid. p. 142

7. Ibid.

8. Ibid. p. 144

9. Ibid. p. 146

10. Ibid. p. 150

Bibliography

❖

AIDS

Bamforth, Nick. *AIDS and the Healer Within*. New York: Amethyst Books, 1987.

Badgley, Laurence, M.D.. *Healing AIDS Naturally*. San Bruno, CA: Human Energy Press, 1986.

Callen, Michael, ed. *Surviving and Thriving with AIDS: Hints for the Newly Diagnosed*. New York: People With AIDS Coalition, 1987.

——. *Surviving and Thriving with AIDS: Collected Wisdom*, Vol. 2. New York: People with AIDS Coalition, 1988.

Cohen, Misha. A *Comprehensive Program for Acquired Immune Deficiency Syndrome and AIDS Related Complex*. San Francisco: Quan Yin Publications, 1987.

Columbia Gay Health Advocacy Project. *AIDS: Improving the Odds 1988*. New York: Columbia University, 1989.

Columbus AIDS Task Force. *Buddy Support Program* (unpublished manual). Columbus,Ohio, 1987.

Delaney, Martin and Goldblum, Peter, Ph.D., M.P.H., with Joseph Brewer. *Strategies for Survival: A Gay Men's Health*

Manual for the Age of AIDS. New York: St. Martin's Press, 1987.

Dessaint, Alain Y., Kerby, Jody L., and McLean, Barbara E., eds. *AIDS: Abstracts of the Psychological and Behavioral Literature, 1983-1988*. Washington, DC: American Psychological Association, 1988.

Frumkin, Lyn, M.D. and Leonard, John, M.D.. *Questions & Answers on AIDS*. New York: Avon Books, 1987.

Hirsch, Michael, with John Gamrecki. *How to Start a Local Group for People with AIDS: A Practical Handbook for Grassroots Organizers*. Washington, D.C.: National Association of People with AIDS, 1988.

Martelli, Leonard J., with Peltz, Fran D., C.R.C. and Messina, William, C.S.W.. *When Someone You Know Has AIDS*. New York: Crown Publishers, 1987.

O'Connor, Tom, with Ahmed Gonzalez-Nunez. *Living With AIDS: Reaching Out*. San Francisco: Corwin Publishers, 1987.

Shealy, C. Norman, M.D., Ph.D. and Myss, Caroline M., M.A. *AIDS: Passageway to Transformation*. Walpole, NH: Stillpoint Publishing, 1987.

Tilleraas, Perry. *The Color of Light*. San Francisco: Harper/Hazelden, 1988.

Understanding Death and Dying

Kubler-Ross, Elisabeth. *Working It Through*. New York: Collier Books, 1982.

Levine, Stephen. *Healing into Life and Death*. Garden City, NY: Anchor Press/Doubleday 1987.

——. *Meetings at the Edge: Dialogues with the Grieving and the Dying, the Healing and the Healed.* Garden City, NY: Anchor Press/Doubleday 1984.

——. *Who Dies: An Investigation of Conscious Living and Conscious Dying.* Garden C'ty NY: Anchor Press/ Doubleday, 1982.

Lukeman, Brenda, Ph.D. *Embarkations: A Guide to Dealing with Death & Parting.* Englewood Cliffs, NJ: Prentice-Hall, 1982.

Healing

Borysenko, Joan, Ph.D. *Minding the Body, Mending the Mind.* Reading, MA: Addison-Wesley Publishing, 1987.

Frank, Jerome D. *Persuasion and Healing: A Comparative Study of Psychotherapy.* New York: Schocken Books, 1974.

Hay, Louise L. *You Can Heal Your Life.* Farmingdale, NY: Coleman Publishing, 1984.

——. *You Can Heal Your Life Audio Study Course* (2 audiotapes). Santa Monica, CA: Hay House, (date?)

Levine, Stephen. *Healing Into Life and Death.* Garden City, NY: Anchor Press/Doubleday, 1987.

Levine, Stephen and Dass, Ram. *Exploring the Heart of Healing* (2 audiotapes). Novato, CA: The Access Group, 1988.

Locke, Steven, MD and Corrigan, Douglas. *The Healer Within: The New Medicine of Mind and Body.* New York: Mentor/New American Library, 1987.

MacNutt, Francis, o.p. *The Power to Heal.* Notre Dame, IN: Ave Maria Press, 1977.

Pearsall, Paul, Ph.D. *Super Immunity: Master Your Emotions & Improve Your Health*. New York: McGraw-Hill, 1987.

Serinus, Jason, ed. *Psychoimmunity & the Healing Process: A Holistic Approach to Immunity & AIDS*. Berkeley, CA: Celestial Arts, 1986.

Shlemon, Barbara L. *Healing Prayer*. Notre Dame, IN: Ave Maria Press, 1976.

Siegel, Bernie S., M.D. *Love, Medicine & Miracles*. New York: Harper & Row, 1986.

Simonton, Stephanie M., Simonton, Carl O., and Creighton, James L. *Getting Well Again*. New York: Bantam, 1980.

Spence, Christopher. AIDS: *The Time to Reclaim Our Power*. London: manuscript, 1986.

Weiner, Michael A., Ph.D. with Kathleen Goss, M.A. *Maximum Immunity*. New York: Pocket Books, 1987.

Imagery

Achterberg, Jeanne. *Imagery in Healing: Shamanism and Modern Medicine*. Boston: New Science Library/ Shambala, 1985.

Bry, Adelaide. *Visualization: Directing the Movies of Your Mind*. New York: Barnes & Nobles Books, 1979.

Gawain, Shakti. *Creative Visualization*. New York: Bantam Books, 1978.

Lazarus, Arnold, Ph.D. *In the Mind's Eye: The Power of Imagery for Personal Enrichment*. New York: The Guilford Press, 1977.

Nouwen, Henri J.M. *Behold the Beauty of the Lord: Praying with Icons*. Notre Dame, IN: Ave Maria Press, 1987.

Rossman, Martin L., M.D. *Healing Yourself: A Step by Step Guide for Better Health Through Imagery*. New York: Walker & Co., 1987.

Nutrition

Ballentine, Rudolph. *Diet & Nutrition: A Holistic Approach*. Honesdale, PA: Himalayan Press, 1982.

Brody, Jane. *Good Food Book*. New York: Bantam Books/ W.W. Norton, 1982.

Colbin, Annemarie. *Food and Healing*. New York: Ballantine, 1986.

Goldbeck, Nikki & David. *American Whole Foods Cuisine*. New York: Plume Books, 1983.

Kirschmann, John D. *The Nutrition Almanac, 2nd Edition*. New York: McGraw Hill, 1984.

Robbins, John. *Diet for a New America*. Walpole, N.H.: Stillpoint Publishing, 1987.

Satchidananda, Swami. *The Healthy Vegetarian*. Yogaville, VA: Integral Yoga Publishers, 1986.

Psychotherapy

Alberti, Robert E., Ph.D., and Emmons, Michael L., Ph.D.. *Your Perfect Right*. San Luis Obispo, CA: Impact Publishers, 1986.

Carrington, Patricia, Ph.D. *Releasing*. New York: William Morrow & Co., 1984.

Davis, Martha, Ph.D., Eshelman, Elizabeth R., M.S.W., and McKay, Matthew, Ph.D.. *The Relaxation & Stress Reduction Workbook, 2nd Edition*. Oakland, CA: New Harbinger Publications, 1982.

Ferrucci, Piero. *What We May Be: Techniques for Psychological and Spiritual Growth Through Psychosynthesis*. Los Angeles: Jeremy P. Tarcher, 1982.

Frankl, Viktor E. *Man's Search for Meaning*. New York: Pocket Books, 1984.

Havens, Leston. *Making Contact: Uses of Language in Psychotherapy*. Cambridge, MA: Harvard University Press, 1986.

Levine, Stephen and Ondrea. *In the Heart of Relationship* (videotape). Novato, CA: The Access Group, 1987.

Rako, Susan, M.D. and Mazer, Harvey, M.D. *Semrad: The Heart of the Therapist*. New York: Jason Aranson, Inc., 1983.

Rakos, Richard F., Ph.D. and Schroeder, Harold E., Ph.D. *Self-Directed Assertiveness Training*. New York: DMA Audio Cassettes Program, a division of Guilford Publ., 1980.

Yoga, Meditation and Spiritual Development

Beevers, John, trans. *The Autobiography of St. Therese of Lisieux: The Story of a Soul*. Garden City, NY: Image Books, 1957.

Bordow, Sita and others. *Sri Swami Satchidananda: Apostle of Peace*. Yogaville, Virginia: Integral Yoga Publications, 1986.

Dass, Ram. *Journey of Awakening: A Meditator's Guidebook*. New York: Bantam, 1978.

Goldstein, Joseph, and Kornfield, Jack. *Seeking the Heart of Wisdom: The Path of Insight Meditation*. Boston: Shambhala, 1987.

Integral Yoga Hatha (90 minute audiotape). Satchidananda Ashram: Yogaville, Virginia 1982.

Integral Yoga Hatha: Beginners II (audiotape). Satchidananda Ashram: Yogaville, Virginia 1982.

Isherwood, Christopher. *My Guru and His Disciple*. New York: Farrar, Straus, Giroux, 1980.

Levine, Stephen. *A Gradual Awakening*. Garden City, NY: Anchor Press/Doubleday, 1979.

Mandelkorn, Philip, ed. *To Know Your Self: The Essential Teachings of Swami Satchidananda*. Garden City, NY: Anchor Press/Doubleday, 1978.

Millman, Dan. *Way of the Peaceful Warrior: A Book that Changes Lives*. Tiburon, CA: H.J. Kramer, Inc., 1980.

Nouwen, Henri J.M. *Out of Solitude: Three Meditations on the Christian Life*. Notre Dame, IN: Ave Maria Press, 1974.

———. *The Genesee Diary*. Garden City, NY: Image Books, 1976.

Satchidananda, Sri Swami. *Beyond Words*. New York: Holt, Rinehart and Winston, 1977.

———. *Integral Yoga*. Pomfret Center, CT: Integral Yoga Publications, ˊ978.

———. *Integral Yoga* Hatha. New York: Holt, Rinehart and Winston, 1970.

———. *The Golden Present*. Yogaville, Virginia: Integral Yoga Publications, 1987.

———. *The Living Gita*. Yogaville, VA: Integral Yoga Publications, 1988.

Teresa, Mother. *Life in the Spirit*. San Francisco: Harper & Row, 1983.

Vanier, Jean. Be *Not Afraid*. New York: Paulist Press, 1975.

Please write to Integral Yoga Publications (Satchidananda Ashram, Yogaville, Route 1, Box 172, Buckingham, VA 23921) for a catalogue of books and tapes by Swami Satchidananda and other yoga masters.

Additional

Cornell, Joseph. *Listening to Nature: How to Deepen Your Awareness of Nature*. Nevada City, CA: Dawn Publ., 1987.

Jampolsky, Gerald G., M.D. *Teach Only Love*. New York: Bantam Books, 1983.

Lingerman, Hal A. *The Healing Energies of Music*. Wheaton, IL: Theosophical Publishing House, 1983.

Massage Your Mate (92 minute videotape). New York: VIEW, 1986.

Index

❖